The Chronicle of San Juan de la Peña

University of Pennsylvania Press
MIDDLE AGES SERIES
Edited by Edward Peters
Henry Charles Lea Professor
of Medieval History
University of Pennsylvania

A complete listing of the books in this series
appears at the back of this volume

THE CHRONICLE OF
San Juan de la Peña

A Fourteenth-Century Official History of the Crown of Aragon

Translated and with an Introduction and Notes by LYNN H. NELSON

upp

UNIVERSITY OF PENNSYLVANIA PRESS

Philadelphia

Library of Congress Cataloging-in-Publication Data
Pedro IV, King of Aragon, 1319?–1387.
  [Crónica de San Juan de la Peña. English]
  The chronicle of San Juan de la Peña : a fourteenth-century official history of the crown of Aragon / translated and with an introduction and notes by Lynn H. Nelson.
      p.   cm. — (Middle Ages series)
  Translation of: Crónica de San Juan de la Peña (Latin version).
  Includes index.
  ISBN 0-8122-3068-X. — ISBN 0-8122-1352-1 (pbk.)
    1. Aragon (Spain)—History.   2. Aragon (Spain)—Kings and rulers.   3. Catalonia (Spain)—Kings and rulers.   I. Nelson, Lynn H. (Lynn Harry)   II. Series.
DP124.8.P413   1991
946'.55—dc20   91-8495
                                                                        CIP

In Memory of

ARCHIBALD ROSS LEWIS

1914–1990

Contents

Introduction   xi
Maps   xx

Early History

Chapter 1
Tubal Was the First Man Who Settled in Spain   1

Chapter 2
The Origin of the Goths   2

Chapter 3
How the Goths Seized and Occupied Spain   2

The Kings of Navarre and the Counts of Aragon

Chapter 4
Concerning the Cruelties Visited upon the Christians
    Remaining in the Land   5

Chapter 5
Concerning the Construction of San Juan de la Peña   6

Chapter 6
Concerning King García Jiménez   6

Chapter 7
Concerning King Fortún Garcés [I, c. 880–905]   7

Chapter 8
Concerning Count Galindo [II, 893–922]   7

Chapter 9
Concerning King Sancho Garcés [I, 905–925] and His Deeds   7

Chapter 10
Concerning King Jimeno Garcés [925–931], Who Died
    Without Children, and His Deeds   8

Chapter 11
Concerning King García Iñiguez [851–c. 880] and His Deeds   9

Chapter 12
Concerning the Miracle of How King Sancho [Garcés I, 905–
    925] Was Born, in What Fashion He Became King, and His
    Deeds   10

Chapter 13
Concerning King García [Sánchez I, 925–970] and His Deeds   13

Chapter 14
Concerning King Sancho [Garcés III, 1000–1035] and His
    Deeds   13

The Kings of Aragon

Chapter 15
Why There Is No Count in Aragon   16

Chapter 16
The Partition of the Kingdoms of Navarre and Aragon, and
    King Ramiro [I, 1035–1064]   16

Chapter 17
Concerning King Sancho [I, 1064–1094] and His Deeds   18

Chapter 18
King Pedro [I, 1094–1104] and His Deeds, and the Capture
    of the City of Huesca   21

Chapter 19
King Alfonso [I, 1104–1134] and His Deeds, and the Capture
    of Zaragoza, Calatayud, and Daroca   25

Chapter 20
How the Aragonese Took Ramiro from the Monastery   31

Chapter 21
In What Fashion the Male Line of the Kings of Aragon
    Ended   40

The Counts of Barcelona

Chapter 22
The Genealogy of the Counts of Barcelona   41

Chapter 23
Count Guifred [I, 870–897] and in What Fashion the County
    of Barcelona Came to Him and His Successors   41

Chapter 24
Count Miró [II, 897–927]   43

Chapter 25
Count Sunifred   44

Chapter 26
Count Borrell [II, 947–992]   45

Chapter 27
Count Ramón Borrell [992–1017]   45

Chapter 28
Count Berenguer [Ramón I, 1017–1035]   46

Chapter 29
Count Ramón Berenguer [I, 1035–1076] and His Deeds   47

Chapter 30
Count Ramón Berenguer [II, 1076–1082]   48

Chapter 31
How Count Ramón Berenguer Gained the County of
    Provence   49

Chapter 32
Count Ramón Berenguer [IV, 1131–1162] and How the Kingdom
    of Aragon Was United with the County of Barcelona   51

The Kings of the Crown of Aragon

Chapter 33
King Alfonso [II, 1162–1196] and His Deeds   53

Chapter 34
King Pedro [II, 1196–1213] and His Deeds   56

Chapter 35
King Jaime [I, 1213–1276] and His Deeds, and the Capture of
    Mallorca and Valencia   61

Chapter 36
King Pedro the Great [III, 1276–1285] and His Deeds   68

Chapter 37
King Alfonso [III, 1285–1291] and His Deeds, and the Capture
    of Menorca   86

Chapter 38
King Jaime [II, 1291–1327] and His Deeds, and the Peace He
    Made with the King of France   88

Chapter 39
King Alfonso [IV, 1327–1336] and All His Deeds   102

Appendix

I. Visigothic Kings of Spain   105

II. Kings of Navarre to 1035   105

III. Counts of Aragon   105

IV. Kings of Aragon   106

V. Counts of Barcelona   106

Notes   107
Index   131

Introduction

Background

Most American medieval history textbooks pass rather quickly over the Crown of Aragon. There are many reasons for this, not the least of which is the traditional emphasis that such textbooks place on England, France, and the Holy Roman Empire. Moreover, the Crown of Aragon was a peculiarly medieval phenomenon and did not survive into the modern era. In the fourteenth century, however, it had reached the height of its power and was the most powerful Christian state in the Mediterranean. It was also enjoying a cultural and scientific renaissance, and the poets, artists, scholars, and musicians of the Crown of Aragon were admired and respected throughout Europe.

The monarch of the Crown of Aragon, Pedro IV, or Pere III, as he was styled in his Catalan territories, carried the titles of King of Aragon, of Valencia, of Mallorca, of Sardinia, of Corsica, and of Sicily; Count of Barcelona, of Roussillon, and of Cerdagne; Duke of Athens and of Neopatria; and Baron of Montpellier; in addition to other dignities. His navies ruled the western Mediterranean and held the balance of power in the eastern reaches of that sea. His consulates were established in all the major ports, Christian and Muslim, of the Mediterranean littoral, and merchants from his realms traveled freely and traded where they wished.

King Pedro had many capitals: Zaragoza, Valencia, Palma, Perpignan, Palermo, and Montpellier, but Barcelona was his particular favorite. During his long reign, from 1336 to 1387, he made the city one of the most impressive and beautiful in all of Spain. Many of Pedro's works still stand there: the great ship-building yards; the churches of Santa María del Pí and Santa María del Mar; the royal palace with its great audience chamber, the Tinell; and the Saló de Cent, the hall he had built for the meetings of the representative assembly. His court was renowned throughout Europe for its splendor and grace. Pedro, surnamed "the Ceremonious," held courtly conduct in high esteem, and the court of Barcelona became a model of polish and refinement. The Crown of Aragon was not known simply for superficial display, however. An awakening of Catalan and Aragonese arts and letters had begun by the close of the thirteenth century and in the fourteenth it blossomed into a golden age. Scholars and artists found employment in the government and on Pedro's many building projects, and they found patrons among the wealthy and appreciative merchants of Barcelona and the other cities of the Crown of Aragon.

Pedro extended his patronage to architects such as Guillem Metge, Pere Morell, and Guillem Albiall; sculptors such as Mestre Aloi, Pere de Guines, Jaume Castalls, and Jordi Johan; as well as painters, goldsmiths, and others. A poet himself, although of mediocre talent, he was willing to recognize and reward talent in others. A lover of the Catalan language, he labored to establish it as a literary tongue. Encouraged by their monarch, Pere March, Jaume March, Guillem de Torroella, Bernat Metge, and others created a school of Catalan poetry that was admired throughout Europe.

King Pedro was also a scholar. Deeply interested in theology, law, history, and science, he promoted the translation into Catalan and Aragonese of numerous works, including the Bible, the Talmud, the Koran, the law codes and astronomical tables of Alfonso the Wise, various annals and chronicles of France and Italy, and such classical authors as Seneca, Palladius, Ovid, Livy, Sallust, and Cicero.

The fact that the possessions of the Crown of Aragon included Athens awakened Catalan and Aragonese interest in Greek antiquity. It was during this period that Juan Fernández de Heredía (1310–1396) completed the first vernacular translations of such Greek authors as Plutarch and Thucydides, and Pedro himself wrote the first eulogy of the Acropolis of Athens. Among the other achievements of the period were the establishment of the universities of Perpignan and Huesca, and Pedro's organization of royal record keeping in such a fashion that the Archives of the Crown of Aragon are today one of the richest and best-kept collections of medieval state papers in western Europe.

The fourteenth century also marked the culmination of an age of splendor for historiography in the Crown of Aragon. The late thirteenth and fourteenth centuries were marked by a succession of extraordinary historical works, known as the "Four Pearls." The first of this series was the autobiographical history covering the period 1174 to 1276 and written or directed by King Jaime I, "the Conqueror." Writing sometime near the end of the thirteenth century, Bernat Desclot recorded in detail the events of the reign of Pedro III, "the Great" (1276–1285). Ramón Muntaner (1265–1336) celebrated the accomplishments of the House of Aragon during the period

1201 to 1327. Finally, the autobiographical history of Pedro himself, written on the model of that of Jaime I, covered the period 1319 to 1366 (with notes dealing with the years 1374–1380) and constituted the last of the Four Pearls.

The *Crónica de San Juan de la Peña*, dating from about 1370, tends to be lost among these historiographic giants, but this was not always the case. Until modern times, *The Chronicle of San Juan de la Peña* was esteemed as the earliest complete history of Aragon, and even now one must recognize that it was considered by its contemporaries as the official history of the Crown of Aragon. Virtually every Aragonese historian until quite modern times relied heavily and often uncritically upon the materials it contains, and some of the most famous and beloved episodes of Aragonese history are based solely upon this source.

The work was one of King Pedro's pet projects. There were many reasons for this. King Alfonso the Wise of Castile (1252–1284) had commissioned a general history of his realms, and a simple spirit of competition dictated that the Crown of Aragon should not remain behind the Castilians in an area that Pedro regarded so highly as history. Moreover, Pedro felt that a general history would provide the necessary context for the history he would write of his own reign. There were also other, political, reasons behind the king's desire for an official history of his realms.

It is true that Pedro was in many ways an enlightened monarch and a true patron of arts and letters. It is equally true that he was also a determined and sometimes savage man of politics, and almost everything that he did served a purpose in advancing his political agenda. When he had ascended the throne, the various states that made up the Crown of Aragon were held together in a loose federation, and it became his fixed goal to unite them under his direct and firm rule. One of the tools necessary to accomplish this task was to clarify the historical processes by which the Crown of Aragon had come into being. Each of his various territories had its own laws and traditions, and the peoples of these territories each had their own ideas of the constitutional status of their ruler and the limits of royal power. In order to combat local claims to traditional "ancient rights and privileges," Pedro needed to establish the historical precedents upon which his royal power was based. Finally, the Crown of Aragon was surrounded by potential enemies, all eager to dispute Pedro's rights to his lands and prerogatives. Pedro needed a clear statement of the historical bases of his rights. All of this required a complete and official history of the realms of the Crown of Aragon, and King Pedro directed that such a history be compiled. The diversity of purposes it was expected to serve predetermined that the *Chronicle* would be a complex work. The reader will soon see that the *Chronicle* is only superficially the history of the consolidation of the realms of the Crown of Aragon. The underlying theme concerns the evolution of the powers and prerogatives of the monarchy itself.

Perhaps as early as 1345, King Pedro sent to the monasteries of San Juan de la Peña in Aragon and Ripoll in Catalonia, each reputed to be the oldest in their region, directing them to assemble materials for a complete history of his realms. The monks of Ripoll simply provided a Catalan version of the *Gesta Comitum Barchinonensium*, a history of the counts of Catalonia written in about 1162 that had been revised and expanded in about 1310. The monks of San Juan, however, undertook the more arduous task of tracing the history of Aragon from the first settlement of the Spanish peninsula to the union of Aragon and Catalonia in 1137. In order to do so, they utilized a wide range of sources. Although they relied heavily on Rodrigo Jiménez de Rada's *De rebus Hispaniae*, written in the mid-thirteenth century, they added data drawn from materials found in the archives of the monastery, family traditions, local legends, archaeological observation, and minstrel tales to produce a rich and colorful combination of history and romance.

These materials, an account in Catalan from Ripoll and an Aragonese compilation from San Juan, were then sent to Barcelona. Additional materials were added there to bring the narrative down to the beginning of King Pedro's reign. All these materials were then collated, apparently under royal supervision, and a single official text was finally produced. Historians dispute the exact steps of this process and argue whether the original complete text was the Aragonese or Catalan version. This debate springs primarily from regional pride and is unlikely to be resolved. What is clear is that, by 1372, royal editors and translators had prepared approved editions in Catalan, Aragonese, and Latin, and King Pedro was sending copies to various parts of his realms as the official history of the Crown of Aragon.

This background must be kept in mind when reading *The Chronicle of San Juan de la Peña*, for it is unlike many other medieval chronicles and can be deceptive. The title, for instance, is a misnomer, since only about a third of the work was compiled in the monastery of San Juan de la Peña, and much of this material was drawn from the Navarrese-born, Paris-trained archbishop of Toledo, Rodrigo Jiménez de Rada. It is not an historical account in and of itself, but a compilation of a wide variety of materials that have passed through a number of hands. To take a single example, the delightful story of King Sancho's horse recounted in Chapter 14 must originally have been a minstrel tale told in Navarrese. Jiménez de Rada may have heard the story a number of times, each time with minor modifications. He recast the account according to his own understanding of it when he wrote it down in Latin, and the compilers of San Juan revised his version when they translated it into Aragonese. It was altered even more significantly in Barcelona when it was translated into Latin once again.

There was ample opportunity, throughout this complex process of compilation, collation, and translation, for those involved to modify and amend the material with which they were working, and there is no doubt that they did so. More than that, the compilers regarded popular stories and minstrel tales as acceptable historical data and included a number of such pieces in their work. What they included, however, was only a small portion of what must have been an immense oral literature. The compilers were not only willing to alter their materials, but were also able to select only those data that suited their purposes. Those purposes were perhaps more political than historical, and the reader must keep this fact in mind. The *Chronicle* often appears a bit disorganized, somewhat confused, or even naive. This is rarely the actual case. It is well to remember that the work was compiled by a number of extremely able and astute men, working under the direction of a monarch who was devoting his life to uniting his realms and consolidating his power. The omissions, inaccuracies, repetitions, asides, and even the romantic tales with which the account abounds, all had their purposes and should not be dismissed lightly.

If there was a single mind that shaped the philosophy that underlay the *Chronicle*, it was that of King Pedro IV. The *Chronicle* was completed only when it had received his final approval, and, although many scholars had worked on the project, the chronicler in the last analysis was the king himself. *The Chronicle of San Juan de la Peña* recounts the history of the Crown of Aragon as King Pedro wished it to be viewed. It is thus not simply a history, but also a political treatise on the origins and constitution of the Crown of Aragon and its monarchy composed by one of the last great kings of that remarkable state.

The *Chronicle* was written during a time of great stress and change, not only for the Crown of Aragon, but for all of Western Europe. The Black Death struck Aragon in 1348, depopulating the realm and disrupting both society and government. The Hundred Years' War spilled over into Spain, depleting treasuries and leading to a long and debilitating period of dynastic civil wars. An economic depression settled over the entire peninsula, sparking massacres of Jews and setting the stage for the rebellions and widespread lawlessness that would mark the fifteenth century. One could

not expect a politician as perceptive as King Pedro not to have been affected
by the calamities of the age and not to have speculated upon some solution
to these problems. This perhaps explains the fact that some of the most
stirring passages in the *Chronicle* are those that describe representative
assemblies and their politics. It may appear strange that a king dedicated to
consolidating royal power should be so fascinated by the workings of
popular government, but it should also be remembered that it was he who
built the great Hall of the Council of the Hundred in Barcelona. It is quite
possible that the basic thesis of *The Chronicle of San Juan de la Peña* is that
sovereign and subjects are interdependent and that security and prosperity
can be secured only if they respect each other and work together for the
common good.

In short, like many medieval works, *The Chronicle of San Juan de la
Peña* may be read profitably on a number of levels. It provides an overview
of the growth of the Crown of Aragon, contains historical data found
nowhere else, offers a number of entertaining and meaningful tales, and
affords an insight into the thoughts and aspirations of one of the leading
figures of the complex political world of the fourteenth century.

Text

King Pedro sent a Latin version of the *Chronicle*, written between 1369 and
1372, to the Cathedral of Valencia in 1372, and the work has remained ever
since in the Capitular Library of the Cathedral. The authenticity of the
manuscript is adequately supported by independent documentary evidence, and it has served as the unique basis of Antonio Ubieto Arteta's
edition of the *Crónica de San Juan de la Peña* (Textos medievales, 4:
Valencia: Anubar, 1964). This translation has been based upon the text
provided by this edition, but both the Catalan and Aragonese texts have
been consulted to resolve ambiguities and fill lacunae.

Notes on the Translation

It is always difficult to determine the appropriate style of translation to
adopt. Three considerations determined the style chosen for the present
work. The first was the great variety of styles present in the *Chronicle* itself,
ranging from legalistic résumés of treaties and endowments, dry and re-

petitious portions of annals, and highly developed romantic tales, complete with dialogue, to gossipy anecdotes, sententious reflections on popular sayings, and paraphrases of published eyewitness accounts. The second consideration was the direct and personal tone of the work as a whole. It is a measure of the ability of the editors that they were able to take the compiled work of so many individuals and give it a personality of its own. The *Chronicle* is presented as if it were written by a single individual with a particularly close relationship to his audience. This "chronicler" often lapses into the first person in commenting on his work to the audience, telling them that a portion of it has grown too long, that he does not really understand the causes of the events he is discussing, noting where he has gotten the information he is using, or telling his readers what he is going to talk about next and why. The third consideration was that the editors clearly expected that the work would be not only perused but also read aloud to a listening audience.

All of these factors suggested that the basic style should be clear, flexible, easily understood, and, for want of a better term, friendly. The pursuit of this goal required a certain amount of syntactical modification. Numerous complex sentences were divided into more easily managed lengths; many passive constructions were converted to active forms; and pronouns and relative pronouns were often expanded to avoid the confusion of complex antecedents. In all cases, however, the sense of the original text was preserved, although a number of existing ambiguities may have been resolved.

This basic style of simple and direct exposition has been modified into modern styles of writing that reflect at least some of the variations present in the Latin text. As a consequence, some portions of the translation are cast in legalistic terms, others in old-fashioned or poetic phraseology, and still others in straightforward narrative. In each case, I have attempted to present an English style that reflects the Latin style of the text. I hope that these syntactical adjustments and stylistic conventions have allowed me to provide a translation that not only reflects the meaning and texture of the original accurately, but also is faithful to the intent of its compilers and translators.

Proper Names

The Hispanic historian always faces the problem of how to present personal and place names. Should one speak of King Pedro, Pere, or Peter; the pass of Panizá or Panissars? I have chosen to reflect for the reader the linguistic diversity of the age by presenting all names in the form proper to their region, except where this would cause confusion. Members of the royal house of the Crown of Aragon constitute an exception, and their names are consistently presented in their modern Spanish form. In any event, care has been taken that a given form is employed regularly.

Notes and Bibliography

The *Chronicle* is a combination of fact and fancy, with a vague and sometimes confused chronology. It is also a piece of royal propaganda, with some facts suppressed, distorted, or misplaced. Sufficient notes have been provided to identify the events under consideration, to maintain a sense of the actual chronology of those events, and to indicate major differences between the version of affairs presented in the *Chronicle* and historical actuality. I have not attempted to provide a full commentary on the *Chronicle*, since such a commentary would of necessity be longer than the *Chronicle* itself.

The reader who is interested in pursuing these matters further will find excellent editions of the various versions of the *Chronicle*, although the present work is the only English translation. The best Latin version is, of course, *Crónica de San Juan de la Peña* (ed. Antonio Ubieto Arteta [Textos Medievales no. 4: Valencia: Anubar, 1961]); the Aragonese version, *Crónica de San Juan de la Peña (versión aragonesa). Edición crítica* (ed. Carmen Orcastegui Gros [Zaragoza: CSIC, 1986]), is out of print, but was also published in *J. Zurita. Cuadernos de Historia* (Zaragoza) 51–52 (1985): 419–569. The Catalan version, *Crònica general de Pere III el Cerimoniós, dita comunament Crònica de Sant Joan de la Penya*, has been edited by Amadeu-J. Soberanas Lleó (Barcelona: Alpha, 1961).

There are English translations of the "Four Pearls" of Catalan historiography: *The Chronicle of James I, King of Aragon* (trans. John Forster [2 vols., London: Chapman and Hall, 1883]); Bernat Desclot, *Chronicle of the Reign of King Pedro III of Aragon* (trans. F. L. Critchlow [2 vols., Princeton, NJ: Princeton University Press, 1928–1934]); Ramón Muntaner, *The Chronicle of Muntaner* (trans. Lady Goodenough [2 vols., London: The Hakluyt Society, 1920–1921]); *Pere III, Chronicle* (trans. Mary Hillgarth and J. N. Hillgarth [2 vols., Toronto: 1980]).

The best introductions to medieval Spanish history may be found in

J. N. Hillgarth, *The Spanish Kingdoms, 1250–1516* (2 vols., Oxford: Clarendon Press, 1976–1978), and Joseph F. O'Callaghan, *A History of Medieval Spain* (Ithaca, NY: Cornell University Press, 1975). Roger Collins, *Early Medieval Spain: Unity in Diversity, 400–1000* (New York: St. Martin's Press, 1983), and Angus Mackay, *Spain in the Middle Ages: From Frontier to Empire, 1000–1500* (New York: St. Martin's Press, 1977), are companion books that offer a number of excellent insights. Needless to say, none of these general studies affords any detained analysis of the Crown of Aragon. This deficiency has been remedied recently by Thomas N. Bisson's *The Medieval Crown of Aragon: A Short History* (Oxford: Clarendon Press, 1986). Although brief and generally concentrated on the period after 1137, this work is an indispensable guide to the subject and provides a useful bibliography.

There are a number of useful monographic studies in English of various aspects of the period, although relatively few of them deal with the Crown of Aragon specifically. A significant amount of material has appeared in the form of scholarly articles. An excellent topical bibliography is provided by Agustín Ubieto Arteta, *Historia de Aragón en la Edad Media: Bibliografía para su estudio* (Zaragoza: Anubar, 1980), although a second edition of this work is badly needed.

Acknowledgments

I would like to express my appreciation to Professor Antonio Ubieto Arteta for his excellent edition of the *Crónica de San Juan de la Peña*, upon which this translation is based; and to the administration and staff of the Archivo de la Corona de Aragón for their hospitality and assistance. I owe a debt of gratitude to the late Professor José María Lacarra for his encouragement of this project as well as for his guidance and friendship over the years. My particular thanks are due Professor Emeritus Arnold Weiss of the University of Kansas for the hours he spent in reviewing this work and the valuable suggestions he offered. I am, as always, deeply grateful for the advice and support of my wife, Carolyn. Finally, I am indebted to the staff of the College Word Processing Center of the University of Kansas for their cheerful and efficient aid in the preparation of the manuscript of this work.

LYNN H. NELSON
University of Kansas

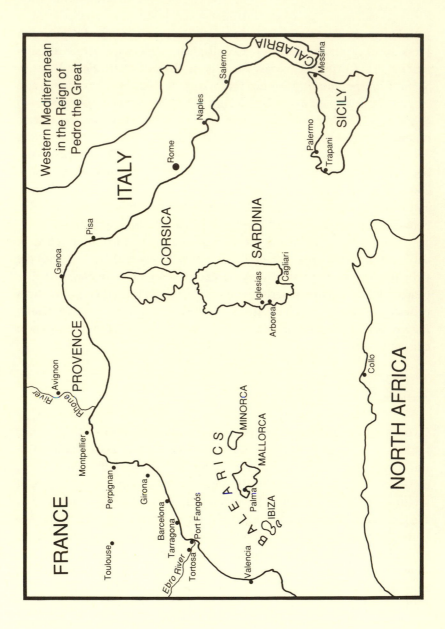

Western Mediterranean
in the Reign of
Pedro the Great

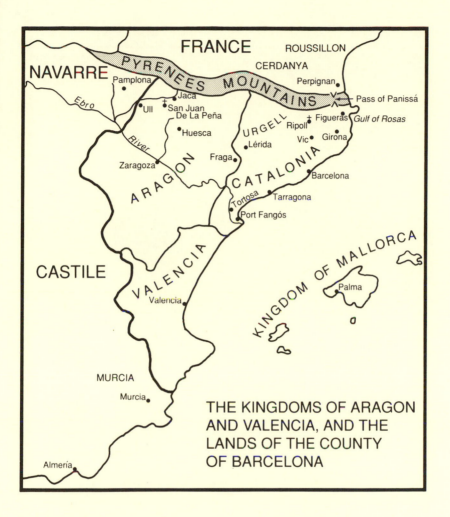

THE KINGDOMS OF ARAGON
AND VALENCIA, AND THE
LANDS OF THE COUNTY
OF BARCELONA

Early History

Chapter 1
TUBAL WAS THE FIRST MAN WHO SETTLED IN SPAIN[1]

According to what we have read in various books, the first man who settled in Spain was called Tubal, from whom the Iberian people sprang. Isidore and Jerome attest to this.[2] From the name of Tubal, they were called the Cetubales. In addition, the land was called Hesperia from a certain star called Hesperus, that shines near the sun between the night and the day. The Cetubales settled on the banks of the river Ebro. Because of this settlement, dropping the name of Tubal, they assumed the name of that river, which is called the Iber [Ebro], and were called Celtiberians. The land that lies between the Pyrenean Mountains and the Ebro River is called Celtiberia.

After this people, Hercules came to rule Spain. He brought to a successful conclusion a war with a great prince named Giron, who ruled the three kingdoms that today are called Galicia, Lusitania, and Betica. Hercules named the first Galicia because he settled it with people whom he had led out of Galatia.[3] He named the second kingdom Lusitana from the river called Ana. On account of another people whom he had led from Cicia to till the land,[4] and because of the river called the Beti [Guadalquivir], he named the third kingdom Betica. The major city of this province was named Ispalis and today is commonly called Seville.

He promptly attacked the province of Carthaginensis and defeated the king of Carpetania, Cati by name, who was quite fearsome in appearance, on the mountain of Carpetania, where he made his home. From the name of this king, the mountain was thereafter called Monticati [Moncayo]. After he had overthrown King Cati, Hercules built a city at the foot of the mountain and populated it with people from Tyre and Ausona who had accompanied him. It is now called Tirassona [Tarazona].

He soon entered the province of Celtiberia. Here he built a fortress that was called Urgell and today is known as Balaguer. He settled a city with men of Ausonia.[5] He named it Ausonia and it is now known as Vich. Later, when leaving that region, he sent out nine ships, eight of which landed in Galicia. The ninth landed on the shores of Celtiberia, where he built a city which he named Barcham Nonam ["Ninth Ship"] and which today is known as Barcelona. This is because it was settled by people from the ninth ship.

In this fashion, Hercules seized all of Spain from the Celtiberians, who remained subject to him. In time, because of the long period of peace, these people forgot the use of arms and neither knew how nor were able to defend themselves. He kept Spain under his power and enslaved to the Greeks.[6] When this had been accomplished, he left, deputizing as governor a follower of his named Ispanus, from whom the country was called Hispania. After Hercules' days, Ispanus was king of Spain and settled many places in the country. He established the city of Segovia, among others.

Chapter 2
THE ORIGIN OF THE GOTHS

In order to be able to deal with matters better, more concisely, and more truthfully, and so that it might be more pleasing for those reading this work to read and for those listening to it to listen (for a long story arouses distaste in both those reading and listening), we do not wish to discourse on Hercules any longer, or on his descendants, or on the people with whom he settled Spain, which he ruled for a long time. It is proper, however, that we discuss the Goths, who came from an island called Stantia,[7] which lies toward the northern regions, next to the sea that circles the world. Claudius and Ptolemy have dealt with these matters more fully in their works.[8]

Chapter 3
HOW THE GOTHS SEIZED AND OCCUPIED SPAIN[9]

The following peoples lived on this island of Stantia: Goths, Visigoths, Ostrogoths, Davirugis, Aretis, and Tanis, all of whom we shall pass over except for the Goths, for it was they who wrested Spain from the Greeks and from the people whom Hercules had established there.[10]

Their first king, with whom the Goths left the island, was named Verig and was a great warrior. When he died, Gaderic, who was a good king, ruled over the Goths. His son Filimer ruled after him. Then Zeuta ruled, and Dianchus and Camoxenus after him. Then Atanaufus, Tlephus, Eurifilius, Voruista, Dizaneus, Diorpaneus, Eumusicus, Estrogotus, and Guina; then Arriachus, Auriachus, Iebarich, and Ermanerich.[11] Then Frederic [Fritigern] and Athanaric reigned and ruled jointly. Athanaric outlived Fritigern and ruled alone. In his days, the Goths came to the Christian faith. Presently, however, deceived and compelled by the emperor Valens [364–378], who was of the Arian sect, they were made heretics and followed the Arian persuasion.

When Athanaric died, the Goths did not wish to choose a king but, on the contrary, submitted to the rule of the Roman Empire, under which they lived for twenty-eight years.[12] Afterwards, however, they chose two kings, Radegaisus and Alaric by name, and refused to obey the Empire. Alaric was the better ruler, and he ruled alone in the kingdom when Radegaisus died. Alaric sought a treaty with the emperor Honorius [396–423], who held the Roman imperium at the time. It suited the emperor to have a treaty with Alaric, and he gave him Spain and Gaul, which is now known as France, to inhabit in peace.[13]

Athaulf, who was the first king to begin to enter into Spain, ruled after Alaric.[14] Enseiaric [Sigeric] ruled after him, and then Wallia, under whom the Goths had their capital at Toulouse. This king seized the lands of Betica and Galicia that were then held by the Alans and Vandals. Theodored ruled after him, then his brother Theodoric, and, after him, his brother Euric. Alaric [II] ruled after Euric, and then his grandson Theudis. Then Theudisclus ruled, and, after his death, Agila. Then Athanagild, Wamba,[15] and his brother Leovigild ruled. This last king enlarged and extended his dominion in Spain. He was also the first to sit alone at table and to wear royal robes, for up to that time all the kings had sat at table with their warriors and had dressed just as they dressed.

After Leovigild, his son Recared ruled. He was a Catholic king, expelled all the Arian sect from his realms, and made Toledo the capital of his kingdom. After him, his son Liuva [II] ruled, and then Witteric. After Witteric's death, Gundemar ruled, and then Sisebut, who compelled the Jews to submit to baptism. In Sisebut's time, Muhammad began to preach his perfidious doctrine in the lands of Mecca and in other territories beyond the seas which are now in the hands of the Moors. After Sisebut, his son Recared [II] ruled, but he died in the flower of his youth. After Recared [II], Suinthila, son of Recared [I], ruled, and he occupied all the lands, cities, and places in Spain over which the Romans held dominion, and he ruled all of Spain without exception.[16] After Suinthila, his son Reximir ruled, and then his brother Sisenand. After Sisenand's death, Chintila ruled, and then Tulga. After Tulga's death, Chindasvinth ruled, and then Recceswinth. After Recceswinth's death, Wamba ruled. He was a Catholic king, virtuous and a great warrior, and extended his realms greatly. After him, Euric [II] reigned, and, after him, Flavius Egica. Then came Witiza, who was a very cruel king. He decreed that the bishops and clerics of the land might keep concubines, and he had the fortifications of all the cities and places of his realm destroyed, so that the people might not be able to rebel against him.

After Witiza, Roderic ruled. He lost his realms in the following manner. Roderic sent Count Julian, one of his subjects, on an embassy to the Saracen King Haboalim. While the count was gone on this royal business, Roderic had carnal relations with the count's wife, according to some, or, according to others, with his daughter, who was in the royal service at he time. When the count returned and learned of these things, he undertook to destroy Roderic's kingdom, and so it was done. On 11 November 713,[17] in the third year of King Roderic's reign, under the direction of Count Julian, King Haboalim, together with Abocubra, king of the Moroccans, King Ezarich, and twenty-five other Saracen kings, invaded Spain. A battle took place between them and King Roderic; the king was defeated and all of Spain up to Arles in Provence was occupied by the Saracens.[18] This was accomplished within fourteen months. These matters, and the struggles maintained since that time, are discussed more fully in the chronicles of Castile in another work.[19]

The Kings of Navarre and the Counts of Aragon

Chapter 4

CONCERNING THE CRUELTIES VISITED UPON THE CHRISTIANS REMAINING IN THE LAND[20]

When this invasion, or subjugation, was complete, the Christians who had been able to escape scattered and fled to the mountain retreats and fastnesses of Sobrarbe, Ribagorza, Aragon, Berroza, Artieda, Ordoña, Vizcaya, Alava, and Asturias. There they built many fortresses and other strongholds in which they were able to protect and defend themselves against the Saracens. All of these lands remained in the control of the Christians, and at no time did the Moors possess them.

The Christians who took refuge in Asturias chose Pelayo as king, as is related in the chronicles of Castile. For this reason, we intend to treat only of the kings of Aragon and Navarre. For a long time these realms were under a single king and were unified in the following manner.

About three hundred Christians who had escaped the hands of the Saracens took refuge in the land of Aragon, on a certain mountain called Oroel, near the city of Jaca. They then settled in a nearby district called Pano, where San Juan de la Peña is now located.[21] There they began to build great fortifications—castles, walls, and ditches so that they might be able to defend themselves against the enemies of the Christian faith.

Before they were able to complete these works, it came to the attention of the emir of Córdoba, Abd ar-Rahman ibn Moncavia,[22] that the Christians were surrounding themselves with great fortresses and defenses in Pano and that, unless they were attacked immediately, the Saracens would henceforth suffer greatly as a consequence. When the emir of Córdoba learned this, he was moved by anger and immediately sent for a subject duke of his, named Abd al-Malik ibn Khatan.[23] He ordered him immediately to join a large force of cavalry and infantry that was has-tening toward Aragon, burning and putting to the torch all places in its path, razing fortifications, and capturing and killing Christians without mercy.

Duke Abd al-Malik, carrying out the king's orders, soon arrived at the fortress of Pano with a force of cavalry and foot. When his tents were pitched in the area of Bocarove, he launched a powerful attack upon the fortress and at length took it by force of arms. No Christian, except the dead and prisoners, left that place, and Abd al-Malik completely destroyed the fortifications, as can be seen today.

Chapter 5

CONCERNING THE CONSTRUCTION OF SAN JUAN DE LA PEÑA

At that time, a holy man named John lived in a cave below a great rock, where he had built a church in honor of God and Saint John the Baptist. He devoutly and piously ended his days there, serving God. After John's death, two brothers, both knights, came from Zaragoza. Pious men and distin-guished in their deeds, one was named Voto and the other Felix. Persever-ing in the Catholic faith and serving God, they dwelled there for a long time, until they were called by God and taken to their celestial home, as is written in greater detail in their *Life*.[24] After these two holy men had been raised aloft from this light, there came another two pious men, Benedict and Marcellus. Following the paths set by their two predecessors, they finished the ends of their lives in a praiseworthy manner, serving God. Because they dwelled there and because of their exemplary way of life, all Christians held that cave in great reverence.

At that time, King García Jiménez and his wife Queen Urraca ruled in Navarre, Count Aznar was master in Aragon,[25] and King Abd ar-Rahman in the city of Huesca. In the Year of Our Lord, 858.

Chapter 6

CONCERNING KING GARCÍA JIMÉNEZ

After the death of King García Jiménez, King García Iñíguez ruled in Pamplona. In the Year of Our Lord, 891.[26]

Chapter 7
CONCERNING KING FORTÚN GARCÉS [I, C. 880–905]

When King García Iñíguez died, King Fortún Garcés ruled after him; in the Year of Our Lord, 903. Aznar [II], count of Aragon, died at this time.

Chapter 8
CONCERNING COUNT GALINDO [II, 893–922]

After Aznar's death, his son Galindo was count in Aragon. He had a castle called Atarés built,[27] and he populated many villages and other places. He also built to the honor of God and Saint John a monastery at San Martín de Cercito in the district of Acumuer. With the permission of King Fortún Garcés, he adorned and endowed that monastery with many lands, both wooded and otherwise, from which the monks of that monastery might maintain themselves in proper fashion.[28]

Chapter 9
CONCERNING KING SANCHO GARCÉS [I, 905–925] AND HIS DEEDS

After the death of King Fortún Garcés, King Sancho Garcés ruled in Pamplona. During his reign, Count Galindo of Aragon died, and King Ordoño ruled in Asturias [914–924]. Ordoño was defeated at that time by a king of Córdoba named Abd ar-Rahman, in the Year of Our Lord, 820, to be precise.[29]

During that period, the Saracens grew bolder because of their victory over King Ordoño and conquered lands up to the city of Toulouse.[30] Because of their fear of the Moors, no one was able to resist them. On the contrary, fleeing and abandoning their homes because of fear and terror of the Moors, the Christians gathered in the cave of San Juan de la Peña as if it were an incomparable refuge.

There were about six hundred Christians together with their wives, children, and all their possessions who gathered in the cave where the church of Saint John the Baptist had been built. They enlarged this and adorned it in various ways to the honor of God and Saint John. Later, after faithfully confessing their sins, with great reverence and with hymns and psalms, they humbly and devoutly transferred the body of Saint John [of Atarés] and placed it in a beautiful tomb above which the name and life of the saint were written in marvelously engraved letters. This tomb was thereafter set among three altars that had been erected there earlier, under the invocations of Saint John the Baptist, Saint Julián, and Saint Basilissa. The Christians, led by yet greater devotion, later placed two more altars there, one to the honor of Saint Michael and under his invocation, and the other to Saint Clement. They then established a monastery in that place, with an abbot named Transirico, and clerics who, of their own free will, for reverence of God and the saints buried there, renounced bodily and worldly desires.[31] The Christians did this so that God and His saints might preserve them from the persecutions that the Moors were attempting to inflict upon them. Each of the Christians built his own dwelling there, and within a short time there was a settlement. They arranged for the monastery to be consecrated by a bishop of Aragon named Iñigo, on the feast day of Saint Agatha [5 February].

King Sancho Garcés ruled in Pamplona for twenty years.

Chapter 10

CONCERNING KING JIMENO GARCÉS [925–931], WHO DIED WITHOUT CHILDREN, AND HIS DEEDS

After the death of King Sancho, Jimeno Garcés ruled with his son García. There is no other record of them, for they died with no ruler or successor surviving them.[32] All and general of the land, seeing themselves remaining without a ruler and the land desolate and without a lord, asked themselves whom they might choose as their ruler. They did not find anyone stronger or wealthier than a nobleman from the county of Bigorre named Iñigo. He had come to the Christians' country to defend them against the fierce and terrible depredations of the Moors, whom he had often defeated and put to flight. On account of his nobility and the courage he had displayed in armed expeditions, and agreeing unanimously with the advice of Count Fortún Jiménez of Aragon, they chose Iñigo as king of Pamplona [c. 816–852].

He was so enthusiastic and eager to wage constant war against the Saracens that he hardly rested, or even wished to rest, a single day without carrying the battle to them. Because of his impatience, he acquired the nickname of Arista. Just as the tip of an ear of wheat burns easily when touched by a flame, so too King Iñigo burned with desire to face the Moors whenever he found that they were willing to stand up against him. He was therefore called Iñigo Arista.[33] He took Queen Toda as his wife, by whom he fathered one son, named García Iñíguez. Iñigo Arista died, and was buried in a tomb in the church of San Salvador de Leire.

Chapter 11
CONCERNING KING GARCÍA IÑÍGUEZ [851–C. 880] AND HIS DEEDS

When King Iñigo Arista was dead, his son, García Iñíguez, succeeded him, and ruled with his mother, Lady Toda. He was generous, good, eager to fight against the Moors, and similar and comparable to his father in noble character. The Christians were considerably strengthened and enriched with land by this time, as a result of the countless victories Iñigo Arista and his son, García Iñíguez, had gained over the Moors.

Also at this time, the Christians who had gathered at the refuge of San Juan de la Peña in fear and terror of the Moors went out from the mountains and reclaimed the lands they had earlier abandoned. As a consequence, the Christians held that cave in even greater esteem.

Count Fortún Jiménez of Aragon, who displayed great reverence for that grotto, one day took the road to visit the monastery, making a pilgrimage, or *romería*, there with a large body of his vassals.[34] When the abbot of the monastery learned of the approach of his lord, he went out with all his clerics in as solemn and seemly a procession as possible to meet the count. When they had greeted each other with honor and reverence, they entered the monastery with joy and gladness, and the count was shown through the monastery by the abbot and its relics were displayed to him.

The abbot and his clerics then begged the count, for the honor of God and out of piety, in consideration of their poverty and in celebration of his visit, to condescend to endow the monastery with lands on which they might pasture their flocks and thus provide for their earthly needs. After he had listened to these entreaties, he conveyed and conceded to them a property called Spelunca de Guallons, located near Oroel, requesting them to remember him and his lands in their prayers and good works. When he had completed this transfer, the count left and went to King García Iñíguez. He told him of the pilgrimage, or *romería*, he had made to the monastery and how, in reverence for the sanctity of the place and the devotion he had for the monastery, he had given the monks this property.

The king was delighted at this account and wished to make a similar visit to the monastery. One day, together with his greater and lesser nobles, and with Bishop Fortún of Aragon, he went to visit the monastery and was received there with honor. He then confirmed the donation the count had made to them and gave them in addition a grove called Avetito, where they might pasture their flocks and provide even better for their needs. He gave five hundred denarii of silver for the mass and in honor of God and His saints. When the mass had been celebrated, and he had heard it reverently, he affectionately asked the abbot and clerics of the monastery to remember him in their prayers and goods works, and to intercede with the Lord Jesus Christ and the saints who had chosen their sepulchers in the monastery. He asked that he might always be given the opportunity and ability to rule and govern rightly and justly the people committed to him, and always to be able to gain victories over the Moors.[35] When he had received the abbot's benediction, he left that place and went to Pamplona.

After a short time, recognizing the many favors granted him by God and moved by reverence for San Juan de la Peña, King García Iñíguez returned to praise God and His saints for the victories he had gained against the Moors. The abbot and clerics of the monastery then humbly appealed to him. They explained that the lands that he and the count of Aragon had given them were causing them much labor and great weariness because they were not able to defend the properties or prevent people from driving their flocks into the woods and pasturing them there. Moved by piety, the king granted them a special privilege: that if anyone should drive his animals, of whatever sort they might be, into those woods, the monks might slaughter those animals and cut off their heads with impunity, and without any fear of appeal or litigation. This privilege applied to cattle and any other sort of herd or flock found in those woods which may have entered those properties without the permission of the abbot and clerics. This privilege was granted in the Year of Our Lord 959.[36]

The king died a short time later and was interred with honor in the monastery that is known today as San Juan de la Peña.

Chapter 12

CONCERNING THE MIRACLE OF HOW KING SANCHO [GARCÉS I, 905–925] WAS BORN, IN WHAT FASHION HE BECAME KING, AND HIS DEEDS[37]

When the king was interred, his pregnant wife Onenga survived him. A tragic event occurred one day while she was passing through the valley of

Aibar. A number of Saracens made a sudden attack upon the queen, killed all of her family, and pierced her through the stomach with a lance. She immediately died from this wound. A very short while afterward, a noble baron of the mountains of Aragon passed through the valley. Contemplating the terrible slaughter of Christians that had taken place there, he saw a baby's hand thrust out of the wound in the queen's stomach. He dismounted, cut open the queen's womb as carefully as he could, and drew forth a live male child, whom he carried away with him and had baptized. He gave him the name of Sancho Garcés and had him reared in an honorable fashion.

For some years, the people of the land managed the government themselves, murmuring and complaining and not without cause because there was no surviving heir, being unaware of the child's survival. One day, the nobles, knights, and people of the land were called together to elect some noble baron as king, and they determined to hold a general assembly to decide the matter. When the noble baron who had saved the child from death so that he might someday be brought to light learned of this, he had the child dressed in shepherd fashion, complete with peasant sandals. When his cousins, friends, and vassals had gathered, and he was fittingly attired, the baron went to the assembly at the appointed hour. Entering the palace where the meeting was being held, he was received with honor by all those who were participating in the discussion. Holding the child between his legs, he cried out in a loud voice, "Barons! Take this child, take off the clothes he wears, and take him as your king, for he is in truth your lord. You all know that his mother, the queen, was pregnant when she died on that unfortunate occasion. I am the one who passed through the valley where she lay slain and saw a baby's hand reaching out through the wound in its mother's belly. And God be praised! I drew the child out alive and without injury from her womb. My kinsmen and vassals who were then present, stand in witness thereof, and if anyone claims to the contrary, let him enter the field of battle, and I will come to do trial by combat with him."

When he had said these things, everyone rose up, shouting "Viva, viva! Because this and none other is our lord!" They immediately removed from the child the clothes in which he was dressed and with great joy clad him in royal garments. On that day, they held a solemn feast in his honor. Because he had come to them clad and shod as if he were a shepherd boy, they called him Sancho Abarca.[38]

He was an extraordinary man and began to fight the Saracens vigorously. He conquered the territory from Cantabria to Nájera, to the Montes de Oca and Tudela,[39] all the plain of Pamplona, and even a large part of the mountains. When he had conquered all the mountains of Aragon, he had many castles and fortresses built there to hold back the Saracens. He had many battles with them, in all of which he emerged victorious.

Once, in the midst of the winter season, when he had stationed himself near the mountains, he learned that the Saracens were holding the city of Pamplona under a very strict seige. Confiding in the grace of Omnipotent God, he crossed the snow-covered mountains with men from Cantabria and others of his realms. Since his men were accustomed to being constantly out of doors, they were slowed neither by heat nor cold. Arriving at dawn and committing himself to God, he attacked the Saracens so fiercely that they were completely defeated, and none escaped to return to his own land. Having gained a great victory and offering praise to God and His saints, Sancho and his men gathered booty from the Saracen camp, and the city of Pamplona stood delivered from the great danger it had faced.

King Sancho Abarca had loyal vassals and sturdy warriors, all eager to battle against the Saracens. They were accustomed, even the knights, to carry short spears and travel on foot. The king and his vassals also sometimes traveled on foot and sometimes on horseback. None of them refused to undertake whatever task he might be assigned. Sancho Abarca always thought about how to obtain victory and honor from the enemies of the faith. He was greatly loved by his vassals for this, particularly since he marched with them like a comrade-in-arms and did not avoid exposing himself to the dangers of battle. When he marched with them shod in his peasant sandals, suffering weariness and fatigue, his men's love for him was great indeed.

He seized many places in Cantabria, among which one is today called Sancho Abarca.

He took Queen Toda as his wife, and fathered by her one son, named García, and four daughters. One, named Urraca, married King Alfonso of Leon; another, called Maria, married King Ordoño; the third, named Sancha, married King Ramiro; and the fourth, Blasquita, married Count Muñoz of Vizcaya.[40] He built many monasteries and churches in the county of Aragon and endowed the monastery of San Juan de la Peña with many goods.

In those days, Oriol was bishop in the county of Aragon and Transmiro was abbot of San Juan de la Peña.

King Sancho Abarca ruled twenty-eight years. He died in the Year of Our Lord, 905, and was buried with honor in the monastery of San Juan de la Peña.[41]

Chapter 13

CONCERNING KING GARCÍA [SÁNCHEZ I, 925–970] AND HIS DEEDS

Sancho Abarca's son, García, survived him as heir and king in the land.[42] He would start to tremble whenever he was about to enter battle, or undertake an expedition, or engage in any other perilous enterprise. People therefore called him García the Fearful.[43] Nevertheless, whenever the world needed the services of a brave knight, he was there.

King García was pious, magnanimous, kind, energetic, and so generous that he never refused anyone anything that was asked of him. Because he marched on foot with the infantry as his father had, was a comrade to his vassals, and sometimes went about in peasant sandals, they called him García Abarca.

In those days, Sancho was bishop of Pamplona, and Fortún was abbot of San Juan de la Peña.

King García ruled well and commendably for twenty-five years. When freed from human affairs, he was buried with honor and proper solemnity in the monastery of San Juan de la Peña.

Chapter 14

CONCERNING KING SANCHO [GARCÉS III, 1000–1035] AND HIS DEEDS[44]

After King García's death, his son Sancho succeeded him. He took as his wife a daughter of Count Sancho of Castile, called Mayor by some and Geloira by others. He established good laws; up to his time, all that was done in the land was decided according to the pleasure of the ruler. It is known that there was, within the county of Castile, another county, called Portell, of which Diego was the count.[45] In the year 893, he established the city of Burgos, and ennobled and distinguished it by populating it with nobles, barons, magnates, knights, and other worthy people. He also altered the route to Santiago, for this road had hitherto passed through Alava and Asturias to avoid the danger of Arab attacks. The count established a new route through Nájera, Briviesca, and Dubinaña and its environs.[46] But, because this is not our purpose, we will leave this matter and return to King Sancho. We will endeavor to continue our discussion of his deeds and those of the others who succeeded him in the kingdoms of Navarre and Aragon.

King Sancho ruled in Navarre and Aragon, in the duchy of Cantabria, and in all of the other lands which his grandfather, Sancho Abarca, had ruled. He ruled Castile and León up to the borders of Portugal by right of his wife, since these lands had passed to her by fraternal succession. Because of his conspicuous integrity and virtue, Gascony submitted to his rule; and he subjugated the count of Sobrarbe, who became his vassal and recognized him as lord. Because of the extent of the lands he possessed and ruled, he had himself called "emperor."

He had three sons by the queen. The eldest was named García; the second, Fernando; and the third, Gonzalo. He also fathered another son, Ramiro, by a noble lady of the village of Aibar.

Because of the general fear of the Arabs in those days, all the warriors used to keep their horses in the rooms or apartments where their wives stayed, so that they might have them close at hand in case the need arose.[47] So it happened that the emperor entrusted to his wife in the fortress of Nájera the care of a horse of his that excelled all other horses in quality, beauty, and other equine virtues. The emperor valued it very highly, relying upon it to carry him to safety if necessary. García, his eldest son, fell in love with the same horse. He wanted the horse to be given to him, and one day begged his mother, the queen, to make him a free and clear gift of it [which she gladly did.] A knight in the queen's service knew that the emperor would be very displeased if his wife gave away his horse. He accordingly advised the queen not to give the horse to anyone if she wanted to avoid her husband's anger. Realizing this advice to be sound and reasonable, the queen revoked her gift to her son. García became very angry at this and convinced his brothers, Fernando and Gonzalo, to accuse their mother of adultery. In their father's presence, García charged that she had been conducting a shameful affair with the knight we have just mentioned. This seemed plausible, because there was in fact an excessive familiarity between the two. García's brothers were not willing to be principal accusers in this affair, but they did agree to support García's defamation of their mother.

Aroused to do this great injustice, García told his father that the queen was behaving shamefully with her knight and that his brothers were aware of it. Readier to believe than to demand proof, the king ordered the queen to be seized and guarded closely in the castle of Nájera. He then called a general court, in which it was decided that her innocence might be established through trial by combat. Otherwise, she would be adjudged guilty and condemned to be burned to death. Ramiro, her stepson as it were, a noble man endowed with great virtue and renowned in feats of arms, considered his stepmother innocent and believed that the charges brought against her were false. He himself came forward and offered to take the field of combat against all men, in defense of the queen. He then made all of the guarantees that are made according to custom in such matters.

As the day of combat drew near, a certain monk, a very holy man, went to the emperor and said to him, "Lord Emperor, if the queen has been falsely accused, you will want to free her and see that those who unjustly defamed her are forgiven." The emperor replied, "That would please me, as long as justice is served."[48] The brothers soon confessed, told the monk that they had accused their mother unjustly, and asked for pardon. The monk immediately disclosed all this to the emperor, who was happy and relieved at the news. He ordered the queen set free without delay and asked her to forgive their children and pardon them of the crime and mischief they had committed against her. She replied that she would agree to do so, but only on condition that their son García, to whom the kingdom belonged by right of succession, should never rule in Castile.[49]

So it was arranged that García should have as his inheritance the kingdom of Navarre and Vadoluengo, Nájera up to the Montes de Oca, and Ruesta with all its villages up to Petilla. Fernando, the second born, was given the entire kingdom of Castile,[50] and Gonzalo received all of Sobrarbe from Troncedo to Matidero, and Loarre and Samitier with all their villages and appurtenances. The queen adopted Ramiro, her stepson, as her son, and he was endowed with the kingdom of Aragon. These lands belonged to the queen as her dowry and *arras*.[51] The emperor confirmed the donation thus made.[52]

On account of the great reverence in which he held the monastery of San Juan de la Peña, the emperor ordained that the monastery, which had been hitherto served by secular clerics, should henceforth be served and ennobled by Black Monks.[53] He established such monks there, bringing them from the monastery of Cluny, of the order of Saint Benedict, which was at that time budding and flowering in the Catholic faith. For this and other good reasons, he graciously endowed the monastery of San Juan with many properties and goods. At that time, Mancio was bishop in Aragon, and Paternus abbot in the monastery.

The emperor died in the Year of Our Lord 1034, and was interred with honor in a church tomb at Oña.[54]

The Kings of Aragon

Chapter 15
WHY THERE IS NO COUNT IN ARAGON

Up to now, we have dealt with events in the kingdom of Navarre and county of Aragon simultaneously. We did this because the count of Aragon was always subject to the king of Navarre. For this reason, it was acceptable that we should speak of all of these things together. But with the partition of the kingdom [on the death of King Sancho], Ramiro held the county of Aragon absolutely and without any subjection. For this reason, he was made king. Wherefore we justly intend to write a chronicle, without any extraneous matters, concerning him and his successors, who successively and without interruption ruled in Aragon.

Chapter 16
THE PARTITION OF THE KINGDOMS OF NAVARRE AND ARAGON, AND KING RAMIRO [I, 1035–1064][55]

When the emperor was dead and the partition of his lands had been effected, King Ramiro reigned in the realm of Aragon because it had come to him, as was said above, by gift of his stepmother, Mayor or Geloira, wife of the emperor. She had ample reason to grant him this favor, because he had freed her from the charges levelled against her, as was related in greater detail in a recent chapter.

In the course of time, Gonzalo, the son of the emperor, ruled in Sobrarbe, Ribagorza, and in other lands conferred upon him by his father the emperor. He had gone out to hunt on a certain day and was treacherously murdered on the bridge of Montclús by a knight of his called Ramónat of Gascony.[56] He was buried in San Victorián [de Sobrarbe]. Since he left no heir, the people of the land found themselves bereft of a lord. They were not able to find another lord as good or worthy as King Ramiro, a mighty man with many virtues, who was Gonzalo's brother, and whose realm lay nearer to them than any other kingdom. It was for these reasons that they selected him as king.[57]

He took as wife the daughter of the count of Bigorre, named Ermisenda but called Galberda by another of her baptismal names.[58] He fathered two sons by her, the elder named Sancho and the younger García, who was bishop of Jaca. They also had two daughters, one named Sancha, who married the count of Toulouse; and the other Teresa, who married Count Guillaume Bertrand of Provence.[59]

He also fathered an illegitimate son named Sancho, to whom he gave the lands of Aibar, Javierre, and Latre, with all their villages, and distinguished him with the title of count. He gave these lands to him with the understanding that Sancho would hold them from him in fief and under his direct lordship, would obey him as a liege man, and would acknowledge Ramiro's successors as his lords under penalty of the loss of those lands. If he should act in any way to the contrary, Ramiro's successors might seize his lands and add them to their own.[60]

King Ramiro was very brave and waged constant war against the Moors, from whom he always obtained victory.[61]

He settled the land with many villages and castles. After a time, because the Moors were very powerful, he entered into a pact and alliance with Sancho, king of Navarre,[62] such that the king of Navarre would have his help in case of need. Because of this alliance, King Ramiro made a gift to the king of Navarre of Ruesta and Petilla, with all of their villages.[63]

García, son of King Ramiro, was bishop in Aragon at the time, and Blasco was abbot in the monastery.

Somewhat later, in the Year of Our Lord 1063 to be precise,[64] King Ramiro besieged a Saracen city called Graus. While this siege was underway, King Sancho of Castile,[65] a kinsman of King Ramiro, with the Cid Rodrigo Díaz and at the head of a great army of Moors, invaded Aragon in order to ravage King Ramiro's lands. He hated Ramiro fiercely because Ramiro was an ally of the king of Navarre. Leaving Aragonese territory and arriving near Graus, Sancho killed his kinsman, King Ramiro, in the sixty-third year of his age.[66] Abandoning the siege, Ramiro's men immediately carried the body of their lord to the monastery of San Juan de la Peña, where they buried him.

King Ramiro reigned for twenty-eight years.

Chapter 17
CONCERNING KING SANCHO [I, 1064–1094] AND HIS DEEDS

After King Ramiro's death, his son Sancho succeeded him at the age of eighteen years. Sancho was later called Sancho Ramírez.

Before we narrate his deeds, we will discuss the king of Navarre. It is known that when King García of Navarre died, he was survived by his two sons, one of whom was called Sancho and the other Ramón. Seduced by unspeakable ambition and fearless of divine retribution, in order that he might rule the kingdom that rightfully belonged to Sancho as their father's eldest-born son, Ramón killed his brother in the Year of Our Lord 1076. Sancho's son, Ramiro, fearing Ramón's malevolence, and suspecting that he might kill him as he already killed his father, fled Navarre and took refuge in Valencia, where the Cid Rodrigo Díaz ruled. The people of the kingdom of Navarre, knowing that no legal heirs could descend from a treasonous lord, and wishing to avoid being subject to such a notorious man, deposed Ramón from the royal dignity which he had improperly and unjustly seized. They elected Sancho Ramírez as king and lord of Navarre. He was then king of Navarre and of Nájera up to Montes de Oca, as well as of Aragon and Sobrarbe. Wishing to erase the name of the traitor in the land, he exiled Ramón and expelled him from his realms and kingdoms.

Sancho Ramírez, eighteen years old when he began to rule, was very brave and able, and open with his knights and subjects. He was neither willing nor able to endure the shame placed upon him by King Sancho of Castile, who had killed his father at Graus for the simple reason that Ramiro had been allied with his cousin, King Sancho of Navarre. Not content with this, Sancho of Castile had seized and occupied a great part of the realms and lands of the king of Navarre. For this reason, Sancho promptly marched against the king of Castile with Aragonese and Navarrese troops. While Sancho was besieging the city of Viana, the king of Castile came with a multitude of armed men, and a great battle took place between them. By the grace of Jesus, Who never abandons those who pursue the truth, the king of Castile was defeated and forced to flee in disgrace upon one of his horses, accompanied by only a few of his men. It is said by some that the horse that he rode in flight was without saddle or bridle, and wore only a halter.[67] Victorious and pouring forth praises of God for such a great victory granted him, Sancho crossed the Ebro, plundering and devastating the lands of his opponents and recovering that which his enemy had occupied of the kingdom of Navarre. He held the Castilians so well at bay that they were unable to find any remedy for his power. The king of Castile then begged Abd ar-Rahman, king of Huesca,[68] to break the treaties between him and the king of Aragon and to make war against Sancho Ramírez. Abd ar-Rahman did this, and immediately invaded Aragon.

The king of Huesca did not remain unpunished for violating his treaties, as we shall discuss below when recounting the deeds of King Pedro, son of Sancho. It was understandable that Sancho should at that time conclude a treaty and peace with the king of Castile that he had previously been unwilling to grant. When he learned that the king of Huesca had broken his treaty, he considered it preferable, like a good and Catholic king, to wage war against the Moors rather than against Christians. Also, he made peace only after having obtained victory and honor from the king of Castile. When he had recovered all that the king of Castile had taken from the kingdom of Navarre and, by the grace of God, had returned that which he had taken from Castile, Sancho Ramírez entered into a treaty of peace with the king of Castile.

He took as wife Lady Felicia,[69] from whom he fathered three sons, Pedro, Alfonso, and Ramiro. Ramiro was a monk of Saint Pons de Thomières. It is known that King Sancho ruled in Aragon for six years before he became king of Navarre.[70]

The Roman liturgy then entered San Juan de la Peña on the eleventh of the calends of April, the second week of Lent, the third feria.[71] The first and third hours were Toledan and the sixth Roman, in the Year of Our Lord 1071. From that time on the Roman rite was observed.

King Sancho Ramírez was a good and virtuous king, which is clearly shown by the following conquests, among other things.[72] In the Year of Our Lord 1080, he took the castle of Corvino and Pratiella, and then the Saracens burned Pina. In the Year of Our Lord 1081, he seized Bolea. In the Year of Our Lord 1083, he took Graus. In the same year, many Christians died in Rueda, he populated Ayerbe, and there was a battle with the Moors at Piedra Pisada on Christmas day.

In the year 1084, the bodies of Saint Indalecio and his disciple Saint James, who succeeded him as bishop of Urtie, which is now called Almería, were transferred with honor to the monastery of San Juan de la Peña by King Sancho Ramírez, his son Pedro, and Abbot Sancho of the monastery, on Maundy Thursday, the nones of April, the fifth feria.[73] On the sixth and after Easter, the king captured Argüedas. On the tenth of the calends of June [23 May], he took Castella and, on the following Saturday [25 May], he fought a battle at Morella.

Recalling that the Cid Rodrigo Díaz had participated with the king of Castile in the death of Sancho's father at Graus, Sancho fought a battle with him at that place, and defeated the Cid in the month of May in the Year of Our Lord 1088.[74]

The King built the monastery of Montearagón, and the canonries of Jaca and Fanlo. In the Year of Our Lord 1089, on the day of St. John the Baptist,[75] the king and his son Pedro captured Monzón. In the Year of Our Lord 1090, the city of Huesca paid tribute to the king, and he was present at Toledo supporting King Alfonso of Castile against the Moors.[76] In the same year, he populated Estella and donated many possessions, including churches and other properties in Navarre, to the monastery of San Juan de la Peña.

In the year of the Lord 1091, he built Castellar above Zaragoza. In the Year of Our Lord 1092, he recovered Santa Eulalia. In the Year of Our Lord 1093, he captured Almenar. He populated Luna in the Year of Our Lord 1094.

King Sancho constrained the city of Huesca so tightly that the king of the Moors promised to pay him tribute.[77] But the Moors secretly sent for King Alfonso of Castile, who had conquered Toledo, to come to their aid against the king of Aragon. They promised to give him double tribute and to be subject to him. King Alfonso, forgetting the assistance given him by the king of Aragon, who had taken part with him in the conquest of Toledo, agreed to the Moors' request. He sent Count Sancho with all of his forces to their aid, and the Castilian army moved up to Vitoria.

As soon as the king of Aragon learned of this, he marched against the count with his men and his sons Pedro and Alfonso. The count did not expect him and was forced back into Castile. Sancho moved directly from this action to besiege the city of Huesca with Aragonese and Navarrese troops, in the year 1094.

One day, when he had ridden around the city on horseback looking for a place through which he might gain entry, he saw a part of the exterior of the wall which was much weaker than the rest. He pointed at it with the index finger of his right hand, saying, "It will be possible to gain entrance into the city through that spot." The sleeve of his mail shirt fell open, and the arm which he had raised was laid bare. Seeing this, a Saracen archer who was on that part of the wall struck him in the right side with an arrow that found its mark through the sleeve of his shirt.

Although he realized that he had been hit, the king let no one know, but immediately returned to his tent and ordered his men to take an oath to Pedro as their king. Everyone was quite astonished at this. When this had been done, he had his son Pedro promise that he would not desist from the siege of the city until he had it in his hands, telling him many things that the future held for him.[78] After encouraging his army, he ordered that the arrow be withdrawn from his side, which it had pierced, and gave up his spirit to the Creator.

His son began to rule in such a praiseworthy manner and was so great a comfort to the army that they did not suffer from his dead father's absence.

The body of the king who had ruled for thirty years was carried to Montearagón, where it was kept for six months and fifteen days. This was done because, if a funeral were held, the men of the army would gather for it and it might be noted by the Saracens, who would draw great comfort from what had happened. When this time had elapsed, Sancho's body was solemnly carried to the monastery of San Juan de la Peña where, with the celebration of funeral rites, it was placed in a tomb in front of the altar of Saint John.

Chapter 18
KING PEDRO [I, 1094–1104] AND HIS DEEDS, AND THE CAPTURE OF THE CITY OF HUESCA

When the funeral and interment of King Sancho had been observed, his men elevated his son Pedro as king on the day before the nones of June of the same year.[79]

Wishing to obey the command of his father, Pedro, with his men, then continued the siege of Huesca from a mountain called Sancho.[80] It was called this because King Sancho had encamped there with his army when he had besieged the city of Huesca. King Pedro pursued the siege with the greatest effort for six months, through May and the next five. King Abd ar-Rahman of Huesca asked for aid from the king of Zaragoza, named Adal-mozaben.[81] Unless he provided assistance, Abd ar-Rahman warned him, after the king of Huesca had lost his land, the king of Zaragoza would lose his own in similar fashion. The king of Zaragoza called upon two vassals of his, Christian counts who were then in Castile, to come in full strength in his service and aid. One of these counts was called García of Capra, count of Nájera, and the other was named Gonzalo. Gonzalo did not come but did send the greater part of his men. Count García came with three hundred cavalry and numerous Christian infantry to serve the king of Zaragoza. There was such a great number of men in the king's army that, when the vanguard was at the village of Zuera and the column in full march, the rear guard was at Altabas.[82]

Count García sent word to King Pedro that he should abandon the siege of Huesca, or neither he himself nor any of his men would escape death, so great were the numbers and power of the Saracens. But the king, like a valiant warrior, set less store upon the size of armies than upon the service of God and the exaltation of the Christian faith.

Meanwhile, one of King Pedro's vassals arrived in camp. Named Fortún, and an exile from the realm, he led with him three hundred infantry and brought ten packs of maces from Gascony. His arrival pleased the king, and he pardoned Fortún's previous misdeeds. He and another man called Barbatuerta distinguished themselves in the ensuing battle.

At dawn of the next day, knowing that the Moors were near, King Pedro and his men prepared for battle. He stationed his brother, Prince Alfonso Sánchez, who was followed by two barons, Castan of Biel and Barbatuerta, in the first rank. He posted Ferriz and Bahacalla, García d'Entrosiello, Lope Ferrench of Luna, Gómez of Luna, and the above-mentioned Fortún with his maces in the middle rank. The king himself, Ladrón, Jimeno Aznárez of Oteyza, Sancho of Peña, and many other fighting men of Aragon and Navarre formed the last rank.

The king of Zaragoza and his army occupied a certain field called Alcoraz, within sight of the city of Huesca. Prince Alfonso and his rank threw themselves so fiercely upon the Moors that they drove them back an appreciable distance. Then King Pedro advanced. Although he might have been in the last rank of battle, he was nevertheless among the first in the clash of arms.

The battle lasted all day, until the darkness of night forced them to stop fighting. Count García and many Christians fell prisoner. The Aragonese were unwilling to kill these men, but they slew any of the Moors they could.

At nightfall, the king of Zaragoza fled back to his city, together with those of his men who were able to escape. Although the Christians may have been worn out by the fatigue of the battle, they did not show their weariness because of the victory they had won. On the contrary, they were again ready on the next day since they believed that the battle would be renewed. But there were no Moors to be seen except the dead and the wounded. They drove the Moors back to Almúdevar,[83] and as many Moors as they met perished by the sword.

On the same day, there was a great battle at Antioch during the great pilgrimage.[84] A certain German knight fought in both battles, and it happened in the following manner. In the battle of Antioch, where he was on foot, he was snatched up by Saint George onto the rump of the saint's horse. When victory in the battle of Antioch had been won, the saint immediately carried him into the battle of Huesca. Saint George was clearly seen there, with the knight riding on the rear of his horse. The knight was left behind by Saint George, and today the church of San Jorge de la Boqueras is located in this same place. The knight thought that the battle of Antioch and the one where he had been left had been the same encounter; no one knew or understood that there had been two battles. But, because he was educated and spoke Latin, the knight was understood by many to whom he recounted this marvel. It is no wonder that the king and the other Christians took great pleasure in this miracle, and gave the knight many gifts.

According to the estimates of those who took part, more than thirty thousand Saracen infantry and cavalry were killed in this battle, compared with about two thousand Christians.

A surprising number of Moors were killed by blows of the maces. The king heaped many gifts upon Fortún for this reason. He was therefore given the surname Maza [mace] and was made a knight. There are many of his lineage in Aragon.[85]

Having poured forth praises and thanks to the Lord Jesus Christ for the victory he had gained, King Pedro returned to the siege of Huesca. After those within learned that the Saracens had succumbed in battle and that King Pedro had been victorious, they were desperate and downcast, and after eight days they surrendered unconditionally. This took place on the sixth of the calends of December.[86]

In the Year of Our Lord 1094, King Pedro received the Cid Rodrigo Díaz in commendation and promised to come to his aid whenever necessary.[87] At this time, the Cid was under attack by King Alfonso of Castile because the Cid had required from Alfonso an oath that no one else of Castile had dared to demand: that he had not conspired in the death of King Sancho, whom Bellido Adolfo had killed at Zamora.[88] At the time of the murder, Alfonso was hated by his brother, King Sancho, and was dwelling with the king of Toledo. Suspecting that Alfonso had arranged his brother's death, the Castilians were unwilling to accept him as king until he swore to the men of the realm that he had not been a party to the death of his brother. The Cid administered the oath, an act that greatly displeased the king. Because of this, Alfonso hated him, and the Cid placed himself under the protection of King Pedro of Aragon.

The Cid then went to the mountains of Cuenca and Albarracín with three hundred cavalry. Here he built a great fortress on the top of a certain cliff which is today called La Peña del Cid. With the assistance of the king of Aragon and of Pedro Rodríguez of Azagra, lord of Albarracín,[89] the Cid then captured the city of Valencia. But when those from beyond the sea [the Almoravids] came to the aid of the Saracens, they came with a vast number of barbarians and, together with the Saracens from this side of the water, they besieged the Cid in the city of Valencia. Being under siege, he entreated King Pedro as his lord to come to his relief as quickly as possible.[90]

The men of Aragon and Navarre and those nobles in the city of Huesca and its district, who were at that time engaged in confiscating the pagans' lands and placing them under King Pedro's control, were wearied by their labors and advised the king not to go to Valencia.

But Pedro was unwilling either to abandon the Cid, lest such a good knight be lost, or to shrink from the service of God. In the presence of all his followers, he promised the messenger that he would be with the Cid in Valencia within twelve days. It therefore came about that King Pedro, with his barons and the knights of Aragon and Navarre who had taken part in the battle of Huesca, left the city defended by a garrison. Fortún Garcés of Biel, son of Castan of Biel, an eager warrior who was the first to bear the sign or arms of the crows and was called the Prince of Huesca; and Ferriz of Lizana; and Pedro of Verga with other knights and infantry were left behind to defend Huesca. Pedro, meanwhile, marched to the city of Valencia with his brother, Prince Alfonso, a man of great boldness and bravery, and they arrived there before the day promised. Pedro, together with the Cid, then joined battle with Luchar, the greatest of the Saracen kings there. They killed him and were victors. Fifty thousand Saracen cavalry and infantry were killed in that battle.[91]

King Pedro was valiant and bold in passages of arms, and did battle against the Saracens many times, always gaining a victory over them. Whatever gold and silver he was able to acquire, he gave to monasteries and to his warriors.

He had a wife, called Agnes, from whom he fathered one son, named Pedro, and one daughter, named Isabel.

He conferred many goods upon the monastery of San Juan de la Peña. He obtained from Pope Urban II [1088–1099] the privilege that the kings of Aragon, and the nobles and knights also, might confer all churches in the lands acquired from the Moors, except cathedrals, or might retain them for their own use and needs. Also, they could levy tithes for the support of churches, as is contained in the privilege which is in the monastery of San Juan de la Peña.[92]

The children of King Pedro died on the fifteenth of the calends of September [18 August] in the Year of Our Lord 1125. In the same year, on the third of the calends of October, King Pedro was liberated from human concerns,[93] at the age of thirty-five, and was honorably and fittingly interred in the monastery recently mentioned.

Chapter 19

KING ALFONSO [I, 1104–1134] AND HIS DEEDS, AND THE CAPTURE OF ZARAGOZA, CALATAYUD, AND DAROCA

King Pedro died without children, and his brother Alfonso succeeded him in the realms of Aragon and Navarre. He was surnamed "the Battler" because there was no bolder warrior in Spain, the victor in twenty-nine battles.

He married Urraca,[94] the daughter of Alfonso, the king of Castile who conquered Toledo. He was therefore the ruler of Aragon and Navarre by right of succession, and of Castile by right of his wife. He created the burg of Pamplona by establishing settlers in a field of his called Orunya, and conceded many privileges to them. He also populated Soria, Almazán, Berlanga, and Belorado. He was called emperor of Spain in the Year of Our Lord 1120.

He conquered Ejea from the pagans and conceded many privileges to the settlers of that place.[95] It was here that he assumed the title of emperor. Many nobles and knights noted for their skill at arms from Gascony and beyond the passes of the Pyrenees had joined Alfonso. They asked him that the churches that might be built at Ejea be dedicated to the work of the French monastery of Sauve Majeur. On the basis of the papal privilege obtained by his brother King Pedro, and as if it were fitting and proper for him to make such decisions, the emperor granted these churches to the monastery of Sauve Majeur, which today is served by Black Monks, and it still owns them. A few days later, he captured Tauste and gave its church to the monastery of San Juan de la Peña. He then populated Castellar with certain men popularly called *almogávars*.[96] Castellar lies above Zaragoza and had originally been populated by his father.

In this year [1118], he besieged Zaragoza with his Aragonese and Navarrese troops, and with Centule of Bearne and Gascons who accomplished wonders all by themselves. Also, the count of Perche, having heard of Alfonso's outstanding reputation, which had spread throughout the world and distinguished him above the other bold knights of the earth, came from France for the service of God and the emperor.[97]

While the Christians were besieging Zaragoza, the Saracens of Tudela launched many attacks against them and against those who were bringing supplies for the siege along the river Ebro and from Castile. The emperor was no longer able to endure this and detached six hundred cavalry to go with the count of Perche against Tudela. The count positioned himself in a hiding place near Tudela, and sent about three hundred cavalry and a hundred infantry to raid, and seize the men and animals, both great and small, that they found near Tudela. When the Saracens of Tudela saw this, they rushed out against the raiders, as was their custom. Except for a few who remained in Tudela, everyone left the city. None of them suspected a trap as they attempted to pursue the Christians. The count and his men left the place where they were concealed without their opponents seeing them and, finding its gates open, entered Tudela. The count entered a great fortress there and posted a garrison in it. He then hurried back to the gates of Tudela, so that when the Saracens returned, they were either killed or captured. No Saracen remained except the dead and prisoners. The emperor was overjoyed when he learned what the count had accomplished and, like a good and pious man, he gave Tudela as an inheritance to the count and his family.[98]

Afterward, the count returned to the siege of Zaragoza, where a great battle was joined between the emperor and his army on the one side and King Almetzalem of Zaragoza on the other.[99] The king of Zaragoza and those who went out with him to do battle were defeated, and those remaining in the city, as if despairing of their lives, yielded the city to the emperor after much dispute.[100]

Wishing to reward liberally those who were deserving, Alfonso gave Centule of Bearne, as his property, the entire parish of Santa María del Pilar, which had belonged to the Christians up to that time.[101] He gave the count of Perche the district where he was billeted, which today is called "Count of Alperche Street."[102]

The emperor won a great battle at Cutanda, in which the count of Poitiers, a gallant warrior, participated with six hundred cavalry, and in which the son of Miramozmelim was killed in company with innumerable Saracens. The popular proverb, "Peyor est quam illa de Cotanda" [It is worse than Cutanda] comes from this victory.[103]

In the Year of Our Lord 1118, he captured Daroca, Calatayud, and Tarazona; places along the entire length of the Borja river; and neighboring parts of Tudela.[104]

After this campaign, the emperor grew suspicious of his wife, Urraca, and upon his return did not wish to keep her.[105] He put her in Castellar above Zaragoza and, leaving her there under guard, marched to Castile.

Some leading citizens of Castile later reunited her with her husband. But as time passed, Alfonso saw that the queen was straying from the path of honesty. Advancing the excuse that there existed a degree of consanguinity between them and that he did not wish to live in sin, the emperor took her to Soria and turned her over to the Castilians. The grade of consanguinity was as follows: King Sancho, called the Great, had two sons, King Ferdinand of Castile and King Ramiro of Aragon. Ferdinand had a son, Alfonso, who captured Toledo and was the father of Urraca. Ramiro had a son, Sancho, who died in the siege of Huesca and was the father of Alfonso, the husband of Urraca. They were thus in the third grade of consanguinity.

When the Castilians learned that Alfonso had abandoned his wife the queen, who was their natural lord, they were very disturbed and distraught, especially since he had once again set aside the queen whom they had joined to him. Coming to the queen, they asked that a court be called and convened so that they might return her lands to her. This was because they had sworn homage to King Alfonso. But however much they had pledged their fealty to the king and emperor and recognized him as lord, nevertheless, having respect for the dues of natural lordship, they unanimously and amicably returned their lands to the queen.[106]

When this had been done, Count Pedro Ansúrez went to the emperor. He was dressed in scarlet, riding a white horse and carrying a rope in his hand, and said to the emperor, "Lord emperor, I have restored the land that you gave me to the queen, my natural lord, to whom it belonged; and I return to you my body, mouth, and hands, with which I pledged homage to you, so that you may perform upon them whatever you may decide to be justice." The emperor was considerably agitated and angered, and wished to proclaim a sentence against him. He withdrew to deliberate the matter with a council of his men. The council decided that the count had acted properly in restoring her lands to the queen and his homage to the emperor, and the emperor was advised to show grace and mercy to the count. So it was done. It is for this reason that, when a similar case occurs in Spain, a similar usage is observed.

In Castile at this time, there was a powerful count, called Gómez of Candespina. When Urraca had first been widowed, a marriage between them had been considered, but did not come to pass because her father, King Alfonso, did not approve of it. Because of this, when the count learned that she had been set aside by the emperor, he had it in his mind to marry her as had been discussed earlier.

He did not bed the queen through matrimony, however, but by another, illicit means. A son called Fernando Furtado was born from this affair. Since the count considered himself sure of the queen and of marrying her, he began to wage war against the Aragonese, who had held the major fortresses in Castile up to that time.

Another count, named Pedro of Lara, secretly tried as hard as he could to win the queen's love. At length, he obtained what he wanted. With things proceeding in such a manner, and with the realm thus exposed to ruin, King Alfonso of Aragon assembled his men into a large army and invaded Castile. He had many reasons for this action: first because the queen and the kingdom of Castile were being poorly governed, and second because the major fortresses of Castile were held by Aragonese.

The Castilians, with Counts Gómez of Candespina and Pedro of Lara, met the Aragonese at Candespina, near Sepúlveda, and ordered their ranks. Pedro of Lara, with the banner of the realm, was posted in the first rank, and Count Gómez, as if he were more important, was in the last.[107] Wishing to possess the queen, Count Pedro abandoned the banner in the first clash, abandoned his men on the field of battle, and hurried to the city of Burgos, where Urraca was staying at the time.

Count Gómez and the other Castilians fought as hard as they could, but were finally defeated. Count Gómez and many others died in battle. A knight of the family of Olea, to whom the banner of the count had been given, held the banner aloft with his arms when his horse was killed and his hands cut off, and shouted, "Olea, Olea!"[108]

Alfonso crossed then the Duero with his Aragonese and marched through Castile, devastating the land.

Alfonso, son of Urraca and Count Raymond of Toulouse,[109] was being reared in Galicia. Urraca had married Count Raymond before King Alfonso of Aragon, back in the time of her father, King Alfonso of Castile. His father-in-law did not really respect Raymond, so that when the count died, the king was unwilling for his son to be the heir to the realm. Instead, while he was still alive, he arranged a marriage between Urraca and Alfonso of Aragon. Because of Alfonso's ability, King Alfonso of Castile wished him and sons descending from him to rule in Castile and to defend it. This was a necessary consideration because of the threat of the Moors.

Because of all this, young Prince Alfonso marched out with the Leonese and the men of Galicia between Astorga and Leon to do battle at a place called Viadongos. After his ranks were ordered, King Alfonso and his Aragonese were victorious in the battle that ensued. The Leonese and Galicians were defeated and thrown into flight.[110]

When Alfonso had been in Castile for more than a year, he lacked sufficient money to pay his Aragonese and Navarrese troops. He was still determined to hold and possess Castile as his own, however, and turned his hand against sanctuaries, churches, and monasteries. He robbed them of their treasures, and sold and made levies against their properties and possessions. However Catholic he may have been, and however much God may have enriched him in victories, it was from these sources that he paid the salaries of his troops. One presumes that his defeat in the battle of Fraga was punishment for the sort of sacrilege he had committed in Leon and Castile.

Having gained these two victories, he returned to Castile, eliminated the allies of Count Pedro of Lara, and captured some of them. The count fled with the queen, and they shut themselves up in Monzón de Campos, near Palencia. The king then returned to Aragon.

Count Pedro began to make his wicked intimacy with the queen public, planning to make her his wife, and proceeded through the realm as if he were king. He offended the nobles and others of the kingdom by these acts. They blocked Count Pedro's marriage to Urraca and began to become his enemies. They sent to Portugal for Prince Alfonso, son of Urraca and Count Raymond of Toulouse, of whom we have spoken and who had been carried to Portugal when he had escaped from the battle of Viadongos.

The men of the realm then chose him as their king.[111] He was displeased with his mother, who should have been leading an honest life, and even more displeased with Count Pedro for making difficulties whenever he could. With the aid of his men, Alfonso expelled Pedro from the kingdom and held his mother in the tower of Leon until she should submit to his will.

Because the fortresses of the kingdom were held by Alfonso of Aragon, each king prepared to gather his men for war. Before the armies were assembled, however, Alfonso of Castile, following the counsel of his prelates, sent an appeal to Alfonso of Aragon worded as if from a son to his father. He asked that the kingdom be returned to him peaceably, since he was unwilling to acquire it by force. He could not reasonably fight for it because he stood ready to aid and serve Alfonso of Aragon as a son aids and serves his father.

Alfonso of Aragon gave thanks to God for the counsel and insight He had afforded his son, Alfonso of Castile. In order to be pious and merciful, he told those who bore the request that, if Alfonso of Castile had done this earlier, he would not have been an enemy or opponent to him; since Alfonso had now asked his favor he was ready to grant it to him. Lest any further dissension arise between the two kingdoms, it was agreed which lands rightfully belonged to the kingdom of Navarre, namely from the river Ebro up to near the city of Burgos, lands that King Sancho of Castile had violently wrested from the authority of King Sancho of Navarre, son of his kinsman, King García Ramírez.[112] Documents were prepared for these two kings and the kingdoms of Castile and Navarre. Each of the kings received signed and well-validated charters. Alfonso of Aragon yielded absolutely the entire land of Castile which had been held for Alfonso of Castile.[113] From this time on, he did not wish to be called emperor, but rather King of Aragon, Pamplona, and Navarre.

Afterward, in the Year of Our Lord 1125, Alfonso gathered his men, among whom were Centule of Bearne, Bishop Pedro of Zaragoza, and Bishop Esteban of Jaca. They invaded Muslim territory in the month of October, wasting and destroying up to the city of Valencia. They then crossed the river Júcar and destroyed Denia, following which they advanced to Murcia and then Almería, which was called Urtie in those times. Encamping at the foot of a certain mountain of that region, they celebrated the feast of Christmas with great joy and plentiful supplies in a place called Alcázar. They then advanced on Granada and subsequently to Córdoba, wasting and destroying as they went. The king of Córdoba, lord of all the Saracen kingdoms of Spain, marched out with all his might to do battle against them at a place called Arinzol.[114] The Saracens were defeated, the king of Córdoba fled, and innumerable Saracens were killed. Certainly there was no king in Spain who conquered so much or wrested so much from the hands of the pagans, or who inflicted so much harm upon them.

After the passage of nine years, during which he gained victories in many battles and returned the land of Castile to its king, and his people were freed from trouble and at peace, Alfonso was resting at Pamplona because of the great heat. Rumors arrived that the Moorish king of Lérida, with an infinite number of warriors, was riding and raiding up to Monzón and throughout that district. The king of Aragon therefore set out for that area, sending a call through the kingdoms of Aragon and Navarre for all his vassals to come to Fraga, where he himself would be present with three hundred cavalry.

The Moors decided to do battle with King Alfonso before his troops should arrive in greater numbers. When the battle had been joined, King Alfonso was killed.[115] His body was carried to the monastery of Montearagón and later interred there. Others say that, overcome by shame, King Alfonso, who had always been the victor but was now the vanquished, crossed over to Jerusalem, but whether he be alive or dead may never be known.[116] Others say that after a time he returned to Aragon and spoke secretly with certain men who knew him.[117] Still others say that he was lost in the thick of the battle and that he was not recognized, and that he, who had always been the victor and was now the defeated, drove himself on through the battle heedlessly, contemptuous of his foes, because of his boldness and eagerness of spirit.

The best warrior in this battle was Gómez of Luna.

The king was, at this time, in the fifty-first year of his age.

Chapter 20
HOW THE ARAGONESE TOOK RAMIRO FROM THE MONASTERY

When King Alfonso was dead, or lost in battle, the realms of Aragon and Navarre remained without a successor for almost a year. The men of the kingdoms appointed leaders and governors, but they were not well defended from their enemies.

They therefore discussed the matter and decided that they would elect Pedro of Atarés, lord of Borja, as their king.[118] Almost all were agreed on this. But with his election as king not yet effected, he began to behave with habitual and excessive arrogance, not considering carefully the favor which the people of the kingdoms intended to show him.

For this reason, many were ill-contented with him and called a general court at Borja. At this, Pedro of Atarés considered himself sure of the election.[119] Among others of the realm, two, Pedro Tizón of Catareita and

Peregrín of Castillazuelo, since they were leading figures in the kingdom and desirous of the public good, attempted to ascertain who ought to reign.

Attendant of the arrogance of Pedro of Atarés, who was already contemptuous of the people of the realm even before they had made him king, they held a conference with many men of the kingdom. They there told them that Ramiro, who was a brother of their lord and a son of the realm, should be king even though he was a monk in the monastery of Saint Pons de Thomières in the region of Béziers.

A charter of the cathedral church of Lérida recounts how Ramiro was placed, as a small child, in the monastery of Saint Pons de Thomières, of the Benedictine order, by his father, King Sancho.[120] Persevering there devoutly and religiously, he was elected abbot of the monastery of San Facundo and Primitivo, of the same order, in Castile.[121] Later, proceeding from good to better, he was elected bishop of Burgos and then bishop of Pamplona. Finally, after his brother King Alfonso had weighed the matter carefully since he objected to Ramiro's being a prelate in Aragon, he was elected bishop of Barbastro and Roda.[122] While in this dignity, and not through any personal desire for honors but only because of the needs of the realm, he was called by the people of the kingdom of Aragon and pressed to become king of Aragon and Navarre.

While the Navarrese had come to the assembly at Borja with the will and purpose of electing Pedro de Atarés king, the Aragonese were united in opposition and blocked Pedro of Atarés's election. They did not admit the Navarrese to their counsels with friendly demeanor, courtesy, and honor as they ought to have done and were accustomed to do. Considering this, Pedro Tizón of Catareita went to the Navarrese with great courtesy, admitted them to the deliberations, and invited them to dine with him. Moreover, having learned the hour at which Pedro of Atarés was in the baths (others say he was washing his head), he went together with the Navarrese to pay their respects to Pedro. But the porters, acting like stupid or unreliable men (as often happens in their case), did not inform Pedro of this or make as a reasonable excuse for him the occupation by which he was detained. Instead, they simply told the Navarrese that they could not enter to see Pedro because he was engaged in other business.[123] The Navarrese were not a little angered at this response and altered their opinion of Pedro. They altered their intention of electing him king as well, saying, "If you will not suffer yourself to be seen by us now, when you are not yet king, how would you act if you were crowned?"

The Aragonese discussed among themselves how they might take

Ramiro out of the monastery and make him their king. They agreed on a date for an assembly to be held at Monzón. When this had been arranged, the entire assembly dispersed. Pedro of Atarés was left without supporters and, either through his own stupidity or because of the answer returned by his porters, was left in disgrace.

Since the business and purpose of the assembly had been suspended, the Navarrese debated among themselves whether it would be advantageous to them to have Ramiro as their king. They decided that it would not. The reason was that, since the death or loss of King Alfonso, the Navarrese had been worried about Alfonso, emperor of Castile, who was planning to besiege Vitoria and certain other places in Navarre. They doubted whether Ramiro would know how to rule a kingdom because he was a cleric and knew better what was fitting for holy orders than what was proper for ruling a kingdom. They also doubted whether he would know how to defend them, since he was inexperienced in arms and military actions, something quite necessary for a king or prince who has realms or lands to defend, losses to regain, or something to conquer for the first time. Such skills are particularly valued among those that they teach a prince.

The Navarrese therefore unanimously agreed with the advice of Sancho of Larrosa, bishop of Pamplona; don Ladrón, son of Iñigo Vélez;[124] Guillermo Aznárez of Oteiza; and Jimeno Aznárez of Torres that they should send for Prince García, nephew of Ramiro, son of King Sancho of Navarre. How he killed his brother Ramón is fully recounted in the chronicle of Sancho Ramírez who died in the siege of Huesca.[125] Prince García was a cousin of Cid Rodrigo Díaz, who reared him in Valencia, and was a bold warrior.[126] The Navarrese sent for him without the consent of the Aragonese. The Aragonese likewise acted on their own in sending for the monk Ramiro, thinking that their discussion with the Navarrese at the assembly of Borja about making him king had settled the matter.

They therefore sent messengers to the Roman pontiff to obtain a dispensation for Ramiro to leave the monastery and succeed to the throne, since there were no others to whom the government of the kingdom might fall. After great deliberation and at the proper time, the Roman pontiff granted this dispensation.[127] One may read in some chronicles that Ramiro was a priest; in others, indeed, that he was not in holy orders.

When the Navarrese gathered at the assembly of Monzón, Aznar of Oteiza and Fortún Iniguez of Let, who were among the greatest men of the kingdom, did not attend. Those who had come to the assembly withdrew in disagreement.

The Aragonese did not delay, and the coronation took place in the city of Huesca.[128] They raised Ramiro as their king and gave him the daughter of the count of Poitiers as wife.[129] Because the Navarrese had chosen a king without the counsel of the Aragonese, hatred and anger sprang up between the two realms. Ramiro was a good king and very generous to his magnates, knights, and nobles. He gave many places of his realm to them, for which reason they held him in contempt. They warred among themselves, and killed and plundered the people of the realm. They were unwilling to abstain from these things at the king's order. He was greatly perplexed how he might save his kingdom from ruin,[130] but he did not dare to disclose this to anyone.

In order to find a remedy for these things, he sent a messenger with a letter to the person who had been his teacher in the monastery of Thomières. It is the custom and rule with the Black Monks that an old monk is assigned to each novice entering the order, and, in accordance with Ramiro's high status, a master of great wisdom and probity was assigned to him. In this letter, Ramiro informed him of the state of affairs in his kingdom and the life of contempt he was leading among the great men of his kingdom, begging his teacher to advise him what he should do about these arrogant magnates.

When his teacher had received Ramiro's letter with great delight, he considered that he could not advise Ramiro how he might do justice to his nobles without acting irregularly.[131] He therefore led the messenger into a garden where there were many cabbage stalks. Wielding a small knife he was carrying and reading the letter that he held in his hand, he cut down all of the larger cabbages in the garden, so that only the smaller ones remained.[132] He then told the messenger, "Go to my lord the king and tell him what you have seen, for I will not give you any other answer."

The messenger was saddened by the fact that he would not give him an answer. He returned to the king and said that his teacher had been unwilling to give him an answer. The king grew very sad at this. Nevertheless, after the messenger told him what he had seen and the circumstances under which he had seen it, the king interpreted the message to himself as follows: the garden might be his realm, and the cabbages the people of his kingdom, and that some chopping was necessary in order to grow good cabbages.

He immediately sent letters to the nobles and knights, and to all the places of his realm, commanding them to be present on a determined day to celebrate an assembly at Huesca. The king spread the rumor that he wished some French master artisans, whom he had employed, to cast a bell in

Huesca, and he wished them to construct it so that its sound would reach to all parts of his kingdom. When the nobles and knights heard this, they started talking on all sides, saying, "Let us go see this foolishness in which our king is engaged." And they said this as if they set no worth by the man who was their king.

When they had arrived in Huesca, the king ordered certain of his confidential servants to arm themselves in his chamber, and he told them what they were to do there. When the nobles and knights had arrived, he ordered them to be called to council individually, one after the other. When they had entered this room, he ordered those inside to be beheaded immediately. Only those who were guilty in their actions toward him were so called. In this fashion, twelve knights and nobles were beheaded before the king dined. In truth, he would have beheaded all the other nobles and knights, except that those who were outside somehow found out what was happening, and fled.[133]

There were five members of the Luna family among the dead: Lope Ferrench, Ruy Jiménez, Pedro Martínez, Fernando and Gómez of Luna, Pedro Vergua, Ferriz of Lizana, Gil d'Atrosillo, Pedro Cornel, García of Biduara, García of Peña, Ramón of Fores, Pedro of Luesia, and Miguel Azlor and Sancho Fontana, knights.[134]

When these were dead, the others who had fled were powerless, and Ramiro's realm remained quiet, and in security and peace.

He then assembled his troops against the kingdom of Navarre, asserting that it was his duty to do so because the Navarrese had chosen a king for themselves, without the consent of the Aragonese.[135]

When the war and battles had dragged on for a year, the prelates, nobles, knights, and commoners of each realm gathered together and agreed that they should elect three representatives from each kingdom, so that there might be peace and concord between them who had always been as one in peace and prosperity. From the realm of Aragon, Caxal, Ferriz of Huesca, and Pedro of Atarés, and from the kingdom of Navarre, Ladrón, Guillermo of Oteiza, and Jimeno Aznárez of Torres were chosen. Whatever was agreed upon and announced by them should be accepted as pleasing and binding everywhere in that region.

These elected representatives finally gathered at a place popularly called Vadoluengo.[136] Having the laws and arguments set forth before them, they agreed upon certain terms and proclaimed them, to wit: that King Ramiro should regard King García as his son, and that King Ramiro should rule all the people and King García all the knights, so that the rancor and hatred that the Enemy of all humankind had produced and instilled between them and their subjects might be turned against the Saracens. Either king might recognize his lands according to the division Sancho the Great had made.[137] This convention and arbitration was approved and agreed upon, and written down as a permanent memorial. They presented it to both kings in Pamplona, and everyone considered it acceptable and good. They praised it and approved it, and a document of this division of the realm was placed in the monastery of San Juan de la Peña for permanent safekeeping, where it rests today.

On the day following this agreement, King Ramiro was received by Sancho of Larrosa, bishop of Pamplona, by the chapter of his see, and by all of the people of Pamplona, who organized a procession of honor for the king. Afterward, King García petitioned that, since King Ramiro was the father and King García the son, Ramiro should give him some possession of which he might be the heir, as a father ought to endow a son. Since it was very much in his heart to implement the agreements, King Ramiro gave García the places of Sarisa, Roncal, Cadreita, and Valtierra as a donation for his lifetime with the additional condition that, after his death, they should revert to the king of Aragon. And Ramiro immediately had García do homage to him for these lands.

After the passage of three days, while King Ramiro was still in Pamplona, it was suggested to King García that he should ask the king of Aragon to release him from the homage he had done for the places that had been given to him, and that, when he was free of his vows, he should rebel against King Ramiro. And, if King Ramiro should refuse to release him, he should hold the king of Aragon in his power as a prisoner. So it was arranged.

A member of the council of the king of Navarre, a particularly fine knight named Iñigo of Aibar, considered this to a be a despicable plan and felt that the king and kingdom of Navarre would be guilty of unspeakable infamy for perpetrating it. He wrote to the king of Aragon by night and revealed the trap prepared for him. Quite disturbed by the news, the king summoned one of his counselors, named Caxal, together with two other advisors.[138] It was decided among them that the king should not await the progress of the plot arranged against him, but should quit Pamplona in the middle of the night with five knights, which he did. He left for the monastery of San Salvador de Leire, leaving orders that all of his men should be with him at the following dawn. This was done.

When the king of Navarre learned of this, he was greatly saddened, concluding that that which he had planned to do was known to the king of Aragon, and that whatever had been done towards peace was now turned to discord. He therefore ordered the men of his kingdom to make ready, considering that the state of war between him and the king of Aragon was now renewed.

When King Ramiro returned from Pamplona, he called an assembly at Huesca, not planning on making war on the king of Navarre, but on how best to provide for the state of the realm. In that assembly, he ordered messengers to be sent to Emperor Alfonso of Castile, son of Count Raymond of Toulouse and of Urraca, daughter of King Alfonso of Castile, who had conquered Toledo, concerning the plot that the king of Navarre had organized against him. He also noted that his brother, Alfonso Sánchez, had conquered from the Saracens the cities of Zaragoza, Calatayud, Daroca, Tarazona, Tudela, Borja, and all the lands adjacent to them, which were nearly as powerful as the kingdom of Aragon. Because they could not be governed satisfactorily, even though they had been conquered, he asked for Alfonso's assistance, counsel, and favor in these matters.

Caxal was named legate and messenger in the negotiation with the emperor. He trusted very much in certain friends whom he thought he had among the Navarrese, particularly in two of the greatest men of the realm. But King García of Navarre spoke with them, saying that, of all things, they should have Caxal captive in their hands, claiming that the council of Aragon would thus be destroyed, since he was its leader. Such was the counsel of the king of Navarre that it came to pass as he wished. Through these two men who were accompanying don Caxal, he was taken prisoner between Cirauqui and Ochorem, near Puente de la Reina.

When King García had Caxal in his power, he joyously discussed with his men whether he should surrender him to death or to ransom, for Caxal possessed great riches. It was decided in this council that he should be given up to ransom, through which the king might obtain two or three hundred knights for the war that he expected to have with the king of Aragon. He therefore asked Bishop Sancho of Larrosa and the chapter of Pamplona to give the treasure of the church of Pamplona to him so that he could have three hundred cavalry equipped for the war and for the defense of his realm. When this was given to him, the cavalry were equipped. And Caxal was redeemed for an immense amount of money.[139] The abbot of San Salvador [de Leire] sold the treasures of his monastery because he was Caxal's intimate friend. Caxal later restored the treasure to the monastery and gave San Salvador all the property he possessed in Tudela.

On that day, King García made Ladrón, son of Iñigo Vélez, count of Pamplona, and created many knights and nobles since he believed that he would have war with the Aragonese. But God, Who aids negotiations and averts evils, intervened so that the war did not occur.

King Ramiro later appointed another herald to the mission upon which Caxal had been going to Emperor Alfonso of Castile. It was soon decided between them, so that the land conquered by King Alfonso of Aragon should not be lost anew, it should be turned over to the emperor, who was very powerful and well able to govern it. Following an act of homage offered to Ramiro that at the end of his days it would revert to the kings of Aragon, it was turned over to Alfonso.[140]

Then, since King Ramiro desired to ensure that no dissension should arise in the succession to the throne of Aragon after his death, a marriage was arranged between Ramón Berenguer, count of Barcelona, a man energetic in all military activities and in the rule of lands and peoples, as well as a discreet man, and Ramiro's daughter, called Petronilla, which was her baptismal name because she had been born on Saint Peter's day.[141] She was later given the name of Urraca in her confirmation and matrimonial arrangements.

While Ramiro was still alive, she was given in matrimony to the count, and the realm of Aragon given to him as her dowry, under the condition that the children descending from King Ramiro's daughter Urraca should succeed to it in turn and that in no case should the realm of Aragon be transferred to anyone except the children descending from his daughter. This act took place in the Year of Our Lord 1137.

King Ramiro gave Count Ramón the realm of Aragon with the following boundaries and borders: on the Castilian side, from that place called Ariza up to Herrera, and from Herrera to Tarazona, and from Tarazona to Tudela, with its villages and castles.

King Alfonso, his brother, had captured Tudela from the Saracens and had given it to the count of Perche as a signal honor. The count gave it as a dowry to his daughter Margarita,[142] who married García Ramírez, king of Navarre. Arrangements regarding these lands were made in accordance with the donation of King Alfonso.

King Ramiro also gave Zaragoza, Calatayud, and Daroca with their districts after the death of the emperor Alfonso of Castile to Count Ramón.

As we have said above, the king of Aragon gave these places to be held by the emperor for all his lifetime with homage and other securities made for them. After his death, the homage and other things which ought to be done for these places to King Ramiro were to be offered to the count of Barcelona.

Toward Navarre, he delimited the realm as follows: from Santa Engracia de Puerto to Bigüezal as far as it is washed by the river Salazar and as it flows into the river Irati, thence to the bridge of San Martín, from that bridge as far as the Irati flows and divides Navarre and Aragon up to the place where it mixes with the river Aragon, thence through the middle of the bridge to the place called Vadoluengo, up to the place called Gallipienzo as far as the river Aragon flows and mixes with the river Arga and flows into the Ebro, a great river, and thence as far as the Ebro flows up to Tudela.

Furthermore, that after the death of García Ramírez, Count Ramón should recover the places of Roncal, Alesves, Cadreita, and Valtierra, which King García held in homage. Ramiro commanded the count not to fail to recover them.

He gave all this realm as his daughter's dowry with the aforesaid conditions. Although he gave the kingdom as his daughter's dowry, he did not relinquish the royal dignity. On the contrary, he remained king for his lifetime and retained dominion over all the churches of his kingdom and over the monasteries of San Salvador de Leire, San Juan de la Peña, San Victorián, and San Pedro de Siresa, saying to the count, "Although I shall confer the realm upon you, I do not give up the royal dignity."

When all of these things had been done and the marriage completed, the king lived for some time as king, leading a holy and laudable life.[143] The count took upon himself a great number of labors in the realm, which he ruled well, as if they were his own properties and estates, and he paid Ramiro that honor and reverence that a son is expected to show his father, so that there was never any dissension between them.

The king ended his days in the royal dignity in the city of Huesca.[144] In his final hours, he assumed the habit of Saint Benedict, in whose order he had been professed at Saint Pons de Thomières. He ordained that his chaplains should have permanent benefices in the church of San Pedro in Huesca and that they should say the office according to the custom of the monks of Saint Benedict, which is still observed today by those holding benefices there. King Ramiro was interred in this church, in the chapel of Saint George, to be precise.

Concerning the lands that King Ramiro turned over to Emperor

Alfonso of Castile, to wit: the places of Zaragoza, Calatayud, Daroca, and Tarazona with their appurtenances that the emperor might rule them as we have said above, it is true that the emperor was unwilling to restore them to the count of Barcelona, nor did he restore them during the count's lifetime.

It was in the time of Alfonso, the count's son, who at first entitled himself King of Aragon and Count of Barcelona, that the king of Aragon recovered the lands and aforementioned places that emperor Alfonso of Castile held under homage, as was more fully discussed above.

Chapter 21

**IN WHAT FASHION THE MALE LINE OF THE KINGS
OF ARAGON ENDED**

We now put an end to this treatment of the kings of Aragon. Because the realm of Aragon lacked a male heir of Ramiro, it passed to the count of Barcelona by contract of matrimony. Now we shall discuss who the first count of Barcelona was, how the others were descended from him step by step, and what their lives were.

The Counts of Barcelona

Chapter 22

THE GENEALOGY OF THE COUNTS OF BARCELONA[145]

Now we shall discuss the genealogy of the counts of Barcelona. In ancient times, there was a certain knight by the name of Guifred, a native of the village of Arrian in the land of Conflent, near the river Tet.

This knight was very rich, well-armed, and most discerning. Because of his nobility and probity, the king of France gave the county of Barcelona to him, who was his man.[146]

Later, when this count and his son, called Guifred el Pilós, were in the city of Narbonne to confer with messengers of the king of France, he had a disagreement with certain of the king's knights. When a certain French knight scornfully tried to stick his hand into the count's beard, the count, moved by anger, drew his sword and killed the knight.[147] The crowd of Frenchmen who were there seized him and would have led him prisoner to the king of France. Wishing to avenge himself for the shame of his capture, he picked a fight with the Frenchmen leading him captive, and they finally killed him near the village of Santa María del Puig.

Chapter 23

COUNT GUIFRED [I, 870–897] AND IN WHAT FASHION THE COUNTY OF BARCELONA CAME TO HIM AND HIS SUCCESSORS

When they killed the count in this fashion, the Frenchmen led his son, Guifred el Pilós, captive to the king of France. When the king was told why they had killed Count Guifred, he was very displeased that they should have killed him for such a reason, saying that this could injure his realm in times to come.

Then the king received the youth Guifred el Pilós, the count's son, and turned him over to the count of Flanders to be reared, commanding that he be treated with the most diligent care.

When the lad, having resided in the count's court for some time, had become an adult, and a daughter of the count had fallen in love with him, he got her pregnant. This fact was noticed by no one except the count's wife, the girl's mother, who shrewdly discerned it. She was understandably saddened in her heart, but in order to avoid the shame and scandal that might arise, she strove to conceal the burden of her daughter's womb as cleverly as she could. She so well kept it secret that no one knew of it. Turning the matter over in her mind, she decided that since this sort of misfortune had occurred, there was no better solution than that the lad who had deflowered the girl should marry her, provided that he could recover the county of Barcelona. Guifred gave his oath that if he did recover the county, he would take the girl as his wife.

The countess dressed him in pilgrim garb and sent him with a certain old woman to his mother in the city of Barcelona. His mother rejoiced at his arrival. She knew him to be her son because of the hair he had on certain parts of his body where people do not usually have hair; for this reason he was surnamed "the Hairy."

After allowing a few days to pass, she called an assembly of the nobles and barons of the land, who had known her son's father and had been faithful and loyal to him. When she showed her son to them, they were filled with delight. Remembering that great wickedness by which his father was killed, they accepted him as their lord on the spot.

When this was settled, all the barons and nobles of the county of Barcelona went with Guifred to a certain place in Catalunya where Salomó, then count of Barcelona and a Frenchman by race, was staying.[148] When Guifred saw him, he drew his sword and killed him in view of everyone. The whole county of Barcelona immediately came under his dominion. While he lived, he ruled it all the way from the city of Narbonne down to Spain.

Once he was lord of the county, he recalled the shame he had brought upon the count of Flanders and his family by making his daughter pregnant while he was living in the count's court and was regarded as a son. Wishing to honor the oath he had sworn to the count's wife that he would take their daughter as his wife if he could recover the county of Barcelona, he sent solemn envoys to France to lead the count's daughter to him as his betrothed. She was brought to the city of Barcelona, where she was fittingly received. Friends of Guifred's wife later arranged that he should be returned to the favor and benevolence of the king of France. Guifred went into the king's presence and received the county of Barcelona from him.

When he had stayed for a long time in the court of the king of France, now with great honor, reports reached him that the Saracens were attacking his land and had conquered almost all of it.

He told this to the king of France and asked his counsel and aid so that he might drive the Saracens from his land. But since the king was occupied with other affairs, he answered that he could not aid him in anything. He did promise that if Guifred could retake the land that he had lost and defend that which remained to him, it would be his and his successors' in perpetuity.[149] Up to then, no baron had held the county of Barcelona in perpetuity, but whomever the king of France wished to do so acted as count for a limited time.

After Count Guifred had received this favor from the king of France, he gathered many men from the king's lands and with them he expelled the Saracens from the county up to the city of Lérida. He then held the land securely in accordance with the promise. In this fashion, Count Guifred held the county of Barcelona free and quit of the power and dominion of the king of France.

When the count had rooted the Saracens out of his lands, he immediately built the monastery of Ripoll to the honor of God, in the Year of Our Lord 888, and generously endowed it with many riches and gifts.[150]

The count fathered four sons from his wife, one of whom was called Radulfo and was a monk of Ripoll and later bishop of Urgell; another, Guifred, died of poison and was buried in the monastery of Ripoll; another, Miró, succeeded to the county after the death of the count; and another, Sunifred, was the count of Urgell [II, 897–950] and became the most distinguished of his sons after Guifred's death.[151]

Count Guifred was a man of great probity and benevolence, and put his land in a prosperous state. He died in the fortieth year of his age, in the Year of Our Lord 912, and was interred in the monastery of Ripoll.[152]

Chapter 24
COUNT MIRÓ [II, 897–927][153]

When Count Guifred had been thus carried away from the midst of things, he was succeeded by his son Miró, who ruled the county well and honestly for eighteen years. He fathered three sons from his wife, of whom one was named Sunifred; another Oliba, who was the count of Besalú, Girona, and Cerdanya; and the other Miró, who was a count and a bishop.[154]

Miró, count of Barcelona, died in his thirty-fifth year, in the Year of Our Lord 929, and was buried ceremoniously before an attendant crowd in the monastery of Ripoll.

Chapter 25
COUNT SUNIFRED

Three sons succeeded Count Miró. One of them was called Sunifred. He was the first-born and succeeded to the county of Barcelona.[155] Another was Oliba, who held the counties of Besalú and Cerdanya as his inheritance. The last was Miró, who succeeded to the county of Girona. While in that place, from a count he was made a bishop. His sons were minors and were put under the guardianship of Sunifred, their uncle and count of Urgell.[156] Sunifred governed the counties well and faithfully. The monastery of Ripoll was rebuilt during Sunifred's guardianship, in the Year of Our Lord 925.

When Sunifred had completed twenty years of guardianship, the sons of Count Miró were old enough that each of them was able to rule his lands. In accordance with their father's testament, their guardian restored their lands to them: the county of Barcelona to Sunifred, the counties of Besalú and Cerdanya to Oliba, and the county of Girona to Miró. Count Sunifred died a short time later, after returning to his county, in the Year of Our Lord 951, and was buried in the monastery of Ripoll.

He was survived by three sons: Borrell, Ermengol, and Miró. While Sunifred, Oliba, and Miró were residing in their counties, Oliba was given the surname "Cabreta" [Goat]. Whenever he spoke with anyone while irritated or felt angry for any reason, he would always move one foot in the manner of a goat trying to paw a hole in the ground. For this reason, people named him Oliba Cabreta. He was great both in wisdom and among the barons of his land.

Count Sunifred ruled the county of Barcelona in an exemplary fashion for twenty-eight years and died childless in his fifties in the Year of Our Lord 964.[157] He was honorably interred at the monastery of Ripoll.

Chapter 26
COUNT BORRELL [II, 947–992]

Since no son survived Count Sunifred, he was succeeded by his cousin Borrell, count of Urgell and son of Sunifred, the uncle of Count Sunifred.[158]

Although Count Sunifred had a brother, Oliba Cabreta, who by law and reason might have succeeded him in the county of Barcelona better than his cousin called Borrell, we cannot discover why Borrell succeeded, but thus we find it and thus we learn it in writings.[159]

Borrell was count of Barcelona and Urgell, and ruled his counties in peace and tranquility for some time. But in his days, in the Year of Our Lord 965,[160] the city of Barcelona was captured by the Saracens. There was great cruelty and pestilence in the land following its capture. Count Borrell immediately gathered nobles, barons, knights, and infantry in great numbers and, with the aid of God, fiercely expelled the wicked Saracens from the city of Barcelona and from the entire land. After the count had recovered the city and lands that had been occupied by the Saracens, he rebuilt the monastery of Ripoll, in the Year of Our Lord 990.

While Count Borrell was still alive, his kinsman Oliba Cabreta died, in the Year of Our Lord 990. Three of his sons survived him: one was called Bernat, who was heir in the county of Besalú; another was Guifred, who succeeded him in the county of Cerdanya; and the third was Oliba, who was a monk of the monastery of Ripoll, and later bishop of Vic and administrator of Sant Miquel de Cuixá.[161]

Count Borrell ruled the county for twenty-seven years after the recovery of the city of Barcelona, and he died in his eighties. He was buried in the Year of Our Lord 993, and was survived by two sons, Ramón Borrell and Ermengol.

Chapter 27
COUNT RAMÓN BORRELL [992–1017]

Count Borrell's son, Ramón Borrell, succeeded him in the county of Barcelona, and his son Ermengol [I, 992–1010] in the county of Urgell.

Count Ramón Borrell, for the exaltation of the orthodox faith and the oppression of the Saracen sect, went to the city of Córdoba against the

Saracens.[162] Arnau, bishop of Vic; Oto, bishop of Barcelona; and Oto, bishop of Girona, as well as many nobles and barons, went with him. Among them was his brother Ermengol. Ermengol died in battle against the Moors, like a brave knight, in the Year of Our Lord 1002 [sic]. Because in this war he defeated an opponent in single combat, he was surnamed Ermengol of Córdoba. One of his surviving sons, named Ermengol [II, 1010–1038], succeeded him in the county of Urgell Barcelona [sic]. After some days had passed, Count Borrell returned honorably and unharmed from the war.

At that time, Bernat Trencaferre was count of Besalú [988–1020]. He was given this surname ["Iron-cutter"] because he was extremely strong and active. The count of Cerdanya was his brother, Guifred [II, 990–1050], who built the monastery of Sant Martí de Canigó, which he endowed with many notable possessions. Guifred fathered five sons from his wife: the first was named Ramón Guifred, who succeeded to the county of Cerdanya [1050–1068] after the death of his father; the second was Guifred Guifred, who was archbishop of Narbonne; the third, Berenguer, was bishop of Girona; the fourth, Guillem Guifred, was bishop of Urgell; and the fifth, Bernat Guifred, was count of Berguedá.

Count Ramón Borrell of Barcelona held his county for twenty-five years, and left this world in his fifties in the Year of Our Lord 1017.[163] He was buried in the monastery of [lacuna].[164] One son, named Berenguer, survived him.

Chapter 28
COUNT BERENGUER [RAMÓN I, 1017–1035]

Count Ramón Borrell's son, Berenguer, was his heir and successor in the county of Barcelona. In Berenguer's time, in an unfortunate accident, Bernat Trencaferre fell into the river while crossing the Rhone and died in the Year of Our Lord 1020. His body was carried to the monastery of Ripoll and was buried there. He ruled his county for thirty-one years [988–1020] and fathered from his wife one son, called Guillem Bernat Gras, who was instated in Besalú as his heir [1020–1052].

Also in the time of Count Berenguer of Barcelona, Count Guifred of Cerdanya died, in the Year of Our Lord 1025.[165] He had ruled his lands for thirty-five years and was interred in the monastery of Sant Martí de Canigó, which he had built.

Also in the time of Count Berenguer of Barcelona, Oliba, bishop of Vic and son of Oliba Cabreta, with a large assembly of bishops, prelates, and clerics, and with great reverence, dedicated the monastery of Ripoll for the fourth time, in the Year of Our Lord 1032, and enriched it with many possessions. He built the monastery church and adorned the main altar with emeralds, sapphires, carbuncles, and other precious stones.

Berenguer, count of Barcelona, fathered three children from his wife. One of them was named Ramón Berenguer and succeeded to the county of Barcelona after the death of his father. Another was Guillem Berenguer, and he was count of Minorisa,[166] ruled the county for his people in a praiseworthy fashion, and died childless. The other was called Sanz Berenguer and was prior of the monastery of Sant Benet de Bagés, because it was not an abbey-monastery at that time, and he was interred there.

This Berenguer, count of Barcelona, never did anything worth relating, but was the least worthy count of Barcelona there ever was.[167] He ruled his county for eighteen years and died in his forties in the Year of Our Lord 1032. He was buried in [lacuna].[168]

Chapter 29

COUNT RAMÓN BERENGUER [I, 1035–1076] AND HIS DEEDS

When Count Berenguer died, his three sons mentioned above survived him. After his death, Ramón Berenguer el Vell ["the Old"] became count. He was a most excellent and virtuous man, and so eminent among the barons of Spain and even among the Saracens that every year of his entire life twelve kings of Spain came to him as tributaries.[169]

In order to amplify his reputation and enlarge justice, he commanded that a general council be celebrated in the city of Barcelona, in which Ugo, Cardinal Legate of the Apostolic See,[170] and bishops, prelates, barons, and nobles of Catalunya participated. With their advice and consent, the count ordained and established those laws that are today called the *Usatges* of Barcelona and are observed in the county.

He fathered three sons from his wife. The first was called Pere Ramón, the second Berenguer Ramón, and the third Ramón Berenguer. The first and second were like the vipers, who kill their mothers at birth. Pere Ramón murdered his stepmother, called Almodis. It is believed in Spain that it was because of this crime that he died childless.

At that time, Ermengol Peregrín [II, 1010–1038] was the count of

Urgell. He was called "the Pilgrim" because he ended his days as a pilgrim to Jerusalem in the Year of Our Lord 1038.[171] He ruled the county of Urgell for twenty-eight years and was survived by one son, Ermengol of Barbastro [III, 1038–1065]. He had the cognomen "of Barbastro" because he took part in the siege of Barbastro [1064], where he performed nobly. He governed his county for twenty-eight years and died in the Year of Our Lord 1065. He had one son, called Ermengol of Gerp [IV, 1065–1092], who was called "of Gerp" because he built a castle called Gerp near Balaguer, from which castle he conquered the Muslim fortress of Balaguer.

While Count Ramón Berenguer of Barcelona was alive, the count of Besalú was Bernat Guillem Gras [Guillem II, "the Fat", 1020–1052], son of Bernat Trencaferre. He ruled the county of Besalú for thirty-three years. While Ramón Berenguer was still living, Bernat Gras died, in the Year of Our Lord 1052, and was interred in his father's tomb in the monastery of Ripoll. Count Bernat Guillem Gras fathered two sons from his wife: Guillem Troyn, who had a twisted and flat nose; and Bernat Guillem [Guillem II, 1052–1066], who succeeded his father in the county of Besalú because he was a benevolent and pious man. Some nobles killed his brother because he was an irascible man.

The count of Cerdanya at that time was Ramón, son of Guifred, and he presided over his county for forty-two years and died in the Year of Our Lord 1095.[172] Two sons survived him, Guillem Ramón and Enric. When Count Ramón of Cerdanya died, his son Guillem Ramón [1068–1095] was his successor. Guillem Ramón had two sons by his wife, Guillem Jordán and Bernat Guillem.[173] Guillem Ramón's brother Enric was the most excellent knight, and fathered two daughters: one was the wife of the count of Pallars, and the other viscountess of Lautres.

The most excellent Ramón Berenguer, count of Barcelona, ruled his county for forty-two years and established his third son, Ramón Berenguer, as his heir. He died in his eighties, in the Year of Our Lord 1076, and was buried in the Cathedral of Barcelona.

Chapter 30
COUNT RAMÓN BERENGUER [II, 1076–1082]

When Count Ramón Berenguer el Vell died, his son Ramón Berenguer succeeded him. As to his virtues, he was exceedingly brave and bold, kind, pleasant, pious, joyful, generous, and of an attractive appearance. Because of the extremely thick hair he had on his head, he was known as Cap d'Estop ["the Towhead"]. He married the daughter of Robert Guiscard, duke of Apulia and Messina, by whom he had a son named Ramón Berenguer.[174]

Count Ermengol of Gerp, the count of Urgell previously mentioned, lived at that time; as did Bernat Guillem [Bernat II, 1066–c. 1100], son of Guillem Bernat Gras, in the county of Besalú; and Guillem Ramón [1068–1095] in the county of Cerdanya.

While Count Ramón Berenguer was ruling the county of Barcelona, his brother Berenguer Ramón was moved by unspeakable wickedness and jealousy because their father had placed Ramón Berenguer in the office belonging by right to the elder son.[175] One day, while Ramón Berenguer was going down the road, Berenguer Ramón killed him, at a place called Pertica del Astor, which lies between the city of Girona and the village of Sant Celoni.[176] All the men under Ramón Berenguer's authority were greatly saddened at his death, especially because it was of such a sort, and they rose up against the fratricide. It had been his ambition to be the count of Barcelona, but they drove him out of the county.[177] He was sent away for his wicked and impious crime and, hated by the entire world, he went to Jerusalem, where he ended his days.[178]

Ramón Berenguer Cap d'Estop governed his county for seven years, died at the age of twenty-five years, in the Year of Our Lord 1082, and was buried in the church of Girona.

Chapter 31

HOW COUNT RAMÓN BERENGUER GAINED THE COUNTY OF PROVENCE

When Ramón Berenguer Cap d'Estop was murdered, the nobles and barons of Catalunya elected his son Ramón Berenguer [III, 1096–1131] as count.[179]

He took as his wife Douce, the daughter of Gilbert, count of Provence,[180] and gained with her the counties of Provence and of Milhau, which he joined to the county of Barcelona.[181] He had a daughter from Douce, whom he gave as wife to Alfonso, Emperor of Toledo, and from whom a most noble lineage had its origin.[182]

The count besieged the city of Mallorca with a Pisan fleet, and at length captured it.[183]

He started many wars with the Saracens and always gained a victory over them. He seized several of their castles and fortresses, and received tribute from the princes of Valencia, Tortosa, and Lérida.

He had two sons by his wife, Ramón Berenguer and Berenguer Ramón.

While Count Ramón Berenguer was alive, the count of Urgell was Ermengol of Gerp, who held the county for twenty-eight years and died in the Year of Our Lord 1092. His son Ermengol [V, 1092–1102] succeeded him in the county and held it for eleven years. He passed from this world in the Year of Our Lord 1102. Because he went to Mallorca with three hundred horses and a number of infantry, he was called Ermengol of Mallorca. He was succeeded as count of Urgell by his son Ermengol [VI, 1102–1154]. He was called Ermengol of Castilla because he occupied himself for a long time on his mother's estates in Castile.

Guillem Ramón was count of Cerdanya [1068–1095], ruled his county for twenty-eight years, and died in the Year of Our Lord 1095. His son, Guillem Jordán, was his heir in the county [1095–1109] and later went to Jerusalem, where he performed many praiseworthy feats of arms. He was extremely brave and was thought to be cruel by Turks, Saracens and other foes of the Catholic faith, who were greatly afraid of him. He built the castle called Arcaz near Tripoli,[184] where he was struck by an arrow from which he died, leaving no children. His brother Berenguer Guillem succeeded him in the county and held it for eighteen years [1109–1118]. He died without children, in the Year of Our Lord 1118, and left the county to Ramón Berenguer, count of Barcelona.

The count of Besalú was Bernat Guillem [III, c. 1100–1111], who held the county for forty years and died while Count Ramón Berenguer of Barcelona was living, in the Year of Our Lord 1111.[185] He was buried in the monastery of Ripoll. Because he died without children, the county of Besalú reverted to the count of Barcelona.

Ramón Berenguer entitled himself Count of Barcelona and Marquis of Provence. He cultivated peace and justice, and ruled his lands for fifty years. While still in good health and sound intellect, he renounced his temporal goods and properties in favor of his sons, Ramón Berenguer in the county of Barcelona and Berenguer Ramón in the marquisate of Provence. He entered the order of Saint Mary of the Knights of the Temple of Jerusalem. Foreseeing the day of his death, which he wished to meet without possessions, he offered up his spirit to the Creator in the Paupers' House in Barcelona in the seventieth year of his age, in the Year of Our Lord 1131, and was buried with honor in the monastery of Ripoll.

Chapter 32

COUNT RAMÓN BERENGUER [IV, 1131–1162] AND HOW
THE KINGDOM OF ARAGON WAS UNITED WITH THE COUNTY
OF BARCELONA

Ramón was succeeded by his son, Ramón Berenguer, a man of particularly great nobility, prudence, and probity, of lively temperament, high counsel, great bravery, and steady intellect, who displayed great temperance in all his actions. He was handsome in appearance, with a large body and very well-proportioned limbs.

This most noble man took as wife the daughter of Ramiro, king of Aragon, called Petronilla and afterwards Urraca, for whose dowry he received the kingdom of Aragon, in the Year of Our Lord 1137.[186]

This count took part in the capture of Almería with Alfonso, king of Castile, and with many Genoese troops who came there by sea.[187]

He entitled himself Prince of Aragon and Count of Barcelona because the Aragonese did not wish him to entitle himself King of Aragon. His son Alfonso did so, however.

This noble man attacked the city of Almería with fifty-two armed cavalry. There were twenty thousand Saracens within the city, and he encamped near its walls. The people inside the city were affected by such great sadness and fear at his, and his warriors', arrival, that he finally captured it, in the Year of Our Lord 1147.[188]

After he had returned from the capture of Almería, he besieged the city of Tortosa with the aid of the Genoese. He gathered two hundred thousand fighting men there, with whom he attacked the city vigorously and at last took it, in the Year of Our Lord 1148.[189] He built a cathedral church there.

In the following year, he besieged the city of Lérida. Ermengol of Castilla, count of Urgell, participated along with the other barons and nobles. After a furious assault on the city, he took it on the same day of the year following that in which he took Tortosa; that is, on the eighth of the calends of November [25 October]. Afterward, in the Year of Our Lord 1154, he captured Fraga and the extremely strong castle of Miravet. Then he captured the wonderfully well-fortified castle of Ciurana and many other fortresses and castles located on the banks of the Ebro, and, at length, the places and lands that lie between Tortosa and Zaragoza.[190] He exalted the Name of God through the three hundred churches that he built in His honor and glory.

This virtuous man, the count of Barcelona, when he learned that pirates had killed his brother, Berenguer Ramón, marquis of Provence, took over the governance of Provence himself, and received a son of the marquis, his nephew, to rear.[191] He ruled the marquisate in a praiseworthy manner. He destroyed the city of Arles, which was opposed to him, and razed many of its towers and fortresses. He confiscated thirty castles of the Baux family, who were his enemies.[192] Later, he built a great castle on boats in the Rhone. He posted two hundred cavalry and other armed men in it, and then had it pulled up the Rhone with ropes. He moored it by the castle of Trencataya, and the garrison, compelled by fear alone, yielded the castle to the count, who immediately had it destroyed. He then negotiated with the emperor of Germany, and succeeded in having the emperor give his niece as wife to Count Ramón's nephew, who then held the county of Provence from the Emperor in perpetuity.[193]

Ramón Berenguer fathered from his wife, called first Petronilla and then Urraca, two sons: Alfonso, who succeeded him in the county of Barcelona and his mother in the kingdom of Aragon; and Sancho, who succeeded in the counties of Rosselló and Cerdanya; and two daughters, one of whom he gave as wife to Sancho, king of Portugal, and the other to Ermengol, count of Urgell.

Count Ramón Berenguer ruled his lands for thirty-two years and died a fifty-year-old in the city of Turin, in the burg of St. Dalmatia, near the city gates, in Lombardy, in the Year of Our Lord 1162, on the ides of August [13 August].[194]

With his death, the land was thrown into great peril, the people wept with loss, the Saracens rejoiced, the poor were desolate, and the clerics sighed. From that hour, the brigand came out of his cave, the robber appeared, the poor man hid, the cleric was silent, the farmers were defenseless, the enemy exulted, and victory fled, until his son King Alfonso accepted the rule of his realm. The body of the count was interred with great honor in the monastery of Ripoll.[195]

The Kings of the Crown of Aragon

Chapter 33

KING ALFONSO [II, 1162–1196] AND HIS DEEDS

When Count and Prince Ramón Berenguer was dead, his son Alfonso, called the Chaste, was made king of Aragon and count of Barcelona. He was called "the Chaste" because he esteemed chastity above all other virtues. He was still quite young at the death of his father,[196] and the realm was in great peril because of his minority. The count of Provence, called Ramón Berenguer after Alfonso's father, from whom he had received great favors and honors in the past, as we have recounted above, came to Barcelona to compensate for the king's youth until such time as he could rule and govern his kingdom by himself. This count governed the kingdom and county ably and helpfully for two years,[197] and instructed and directed the king so that he might better be able to rule and govern his lands firmly.

After this period of two years, matters arose in his county of Provence such that he had to leave the rule of the kingdom and county and return to his own land. He fought a battle here against the men of Nice, and was so gravely wounded that he died, in the Year of Our Lord 1166. He left no children, because of which he was succeeded in the county of Provence by King Alfonso, although he was then still a child. While King Alfonso was still in his minority, Count Raymond of Toulouse inflicted many injuries upon him but, with the passage of time, Raymond did not escape punishment for them.[198]

King Alfonso was bold and able in military affairs, and recovered Zaragoza, Daroca, and Tarazona with their appurtenances, which the Emperor Alfonso of Castile had held during his lifetime under homage to the king of Aragon, as was discussed in the chronicle of Ramiro,[199] grandfather of Alfonso of Aragon. He recovered these lands and places in the following fashion. When the Emperor Alfonso of Castile was at war with the Saracens on several fronts and was unable to hold them back, he sent heralds to King

Alfonso of Aragon, asking him to come to his aid. The king of Aragon came immediately and, with armed cavalry and brave infantry, participated with Alfonso of Castile in the siege of Cuenca.[200] The emperor was filled with delight at his arrival and thought himself well-supported by such a king and by the warriors he had brought with him. King Alfonso of Aragon immediately asked the emperor to restore those places and lands which he held in Aragon and absolve those who held fortresses and other places for him from the homage they had offered him.[201] The emperor gave his assent to the herald and arranged affairs so that the king of Aragon would remain at the siege of the city, which he finally recaptured for the emperor of Castile. Meanwhile, the emperor retired to assist other parts of Castile that were under attack by the Saracens. Both of them gained great triumphs over the enemies of the Faith.

This king married Sancha, daughter of Alfonso, the great Emperor of Castile, who built the monastery of Sigena.[202]

Alfonso repopulated Teruel, and joined the counties of Rosselló and Pallars to that of Barcelona.[203]

King Alfonso planned to go to the county of Provence for a visit and to stay in the castle of Albanyo,[204] where Hugo, archbishop of Tarragona, and Pere, bishop of Vic, were lodging and resting. Count Raymond of Toulouse, not content with the injuries he had already caused, seized the castle from the king. Following God's Will, Bertrand Baus immediately came to Alfonso's aid, and he and the king mounted their horses together, crossed the Rhone, and reached the city of Arles, where the king was received with honor.[205] Bertrand surrendered a great part of the county of Provence to the king and immediately received dominion over the county, which he ruled generously and firmly as long as he lived. He populated many castles there, among which was one called Colio. Later, when the king was ruling in his kingdom and counties, Bertrand was killed by certain traitors on Easter Day, the Resurrection of Our Lord. His body was carried to the church of Maguelonne, where he was interred, in the Year of Our Lord 1181.

King Alfonso was very much angered and saddened by his death. Mindful of the services that Bertrand had performed for him, and unwilling to be thought guilty of ingratitude, he resolved to avenge Bertrand's death. He besieged a castle called Moruel, where the traitors were who killed Bertrand. At length, he captured it by force of arms and had the traitors put to the sword. They had subjugated many castles of Provence to their own obedience, and he immediately retook the whole land, which he ruled peacefully and firmly as long as he lived.

Alfonso was unwilling to ignore or let pass unnoticed the injuries inflicted upon him by Count Raymond of Toulouse. He gathered cavalry and infantry in goodly number and, impatient of delay, went boldly to the city of Toulouse with his banner flying, destroying the places and wasting the lands of the count of Toulouse. He remained before the city of Toulouse for several days, waiting to see if the count would come out and fight, but the count was unwilling to do so. The king then withdrew and went to the king of England in order to confer with him.[206] On his return, he made his way through the count's land, burning and destroying it. He again remained several days before the city of Toulouse to the shame and dishonor of the count of Toulouse. Retiring from that place at a slow pace, he returned to his own lands with honor.

He then waged war against all the Spanish kings, over whom he always gained victory with honor. He waged many wars against the king of Castile in particular, and once he ravaged and devastated a large part of Castile, which he had invaded with a great army. The king of Castile was very angry and gathered a large number of cavalry and foot soldiers. Coming to the town of Soria, he invaded the lands of the king of Aragon, capturing and putting to death men and women, flocks, and whatever else he could lay his hands on. When this reached the ears of the king of Aragon, he was on his way toward the enemy after only a brief delay. He did not rest either by night or day until he was near them. Seizing a favorable opportunity, he attacked the Castilians furiously and overcame them. In addition to those killed, four thousand were taken prisoner, and he stripped from them whatever they had. With this great victory he returned to the place from which he had come.[207]

King Alfonso had three sons and three daughters by his wife: Pedro, who succeeded to the kingdom of Aragon and the counties of Barcelona, Besalú, Cerdanya, Rosselló, and Pallars after him; Alfonso, who succeeded to the county of Provence; and Fernando, who was abbot of Montearagón. One of the daughters was called Constanza, and was the wife of the king of Hungary. Constanza returned to Aragon because the king of Hungary soon died.[208] Another was called Eleanora, and the last Sancha.[209]

Because of the discord that existed between the Christian kings of Spain, some of them made truces with the Saracens and entered into alliances with them. For this reason, Pope Celestine [III, 1191–1198], desiring that there be peace and love among the Christian kings and princes, ordered King Alfonso and the other kings of Spain not to make peace or truces with the Saracens, but rather to unite as amicably as possible and turn against the Saracens the wars that they were waging against each other. When King Alfonso received this apostolic command, he determined in his heart and vowed in reverence to God to make a journey to Santiago de Compostela.[210] While making his pilgrimage, he negotiated peace and concord among the Christian kings of Spain through his emissaries. While making that pilgrimage, he sowed peace and harmony among them, where discord had ruled before. The greatest honor was shown to him by those with whom he became acquainted. The king did this to please God and obey the apostolic commands. He was unable to unite all of the rulers but in large measure brought them into harmony.

He then returned to his own land, where he found such a great want prevailing that the people were dying of famine, a famine that prevailed in almost the entire world.[211] Moved by compassion and mercy, and in reverence of God, the king proceeded through his lands, distributing food to people about to perish from hunger. Traveling through his lands in this fashion, he came to the town of Perpignan, where he held a conference with the nobles and barons of Provence.

The count of Urgell at that time was Ermengol [VII, 1154–1184], who was killed along with his brother, Gauceran of Sales, by Christians in the city of Valencia, in the Year of Our Lord 1184.[212]

After some time had passed, the king was in Perpignan, confined by a grave illness, and made his testament, in which he named Pedro as his heir in the kingdom of Aragon and the counties of Barcelona, Besalú, Rosselló, and Cerdanya, and his son Alfonso in the county of Provence.

In the forty-second year of his age, he gloriously departed this life, in the Year of Our Lord 1196.[213] He had reigned for thirty-four years, eight months, and eighteen days.

Chapter 34
KING PEDRO [II, 1196–1213] AND HIS DEEDS

King Alfonso's son, Pedro el Católico, reigned after him in the kingdom and counties named above. He was surnamed "the Catholic" because he was a supporter of the Church.[214]

The king's younger son, Alfonso, succeeded to the county of Provence [II, 1196–1209]. This very noble man married the niece of the count of Forcalquier, from whom he had a son called Ramón Berenguer [V, 1209–1245], who succeeded him as count of Provence.

King Pedro was a very courtly man and noble in all his actions. He gave so abundantly of whatever he possessed that he mortgaged and pawned several of his castles, villages, and rents so that he might do whatever was in his heart to do.[215]

He bestowed his three sisters in marriage in the following fashion. He gave the first, who was called Constanza, to Frederick, king of Sicily, who became the emperor of Germany shortly afterward. He had from her a son called Henry, who died in the city of Palermo. Henry, when he was an adult, married the daughter of the duke of Austria. It was said that, because Henry rebelled against his father the Emperor Frederick, he was placed in a prison by Frederick's command. He ended his days in imprisonment, leaving behind no children. Pedro gave his second sister, called Eleanora, to Raymond, count of Toulouse, from whom no children survived. The third, called Sancha, he gave to the son of the count of Toulouse. They had a daughter who became the wife of Count Alphonse of Poitiers, brother of Louis, king of France.[216]

King Pedro married the daughter of the distinguished Prince Guillaume of Montpellier, granddaughter of the emperor of Constantinople.[217] She was called Marie, and he had a son, Jaime, by her. By this marriage, the barony of Montpellier came to the king of Aragon.

Desiring to enlarge the fame of his name, King Pedro went to Rome and most piously and honorably visited the sanctuaries of the Apostles.[218] This was in the time of the well-remembered Pope Innocent III. Esteeming Pedro's integrity of character, the pope crowned and anointed him in the church of Saint Pancras.[219] The king, in praise and honor of God and the Most Holy Roman Church, then returned to his lord the Supreme Pontiff and to the Church the right of patronage which he enjoyed over all the churches established within his dominions. Up to then, neither the Supreme Pontiff nor any other prelate could confer any church established in the kingdom of Aragon without the consent of the king.[220] In consideration of this remission, the Roman pontiff ordained in honor of the House of Aragon that he himself and all his successors would carry a banner emblazoned with the emblems and arms of the king of Aragon.

When the king returned to Aragon, the nobles and knights of Aragon informed him that the remission and donation that he had made to the Lord Pope was invalid because the privilege the king enjoyed over the churches of Aragon extended to them also, over the churches built in their lands. The king answered that he had remitted to the Lord Pope his right, not theirs. They protested his action. The statement of this privilege that the king, nobles, and barons have of conferring churches is in the monastery of San Juan de la Peña, where they keep it because it is an original.[221]

When these matters were ended, the king journeyed to Provence. While he was there, he learned that the count of Forcalquier had taken his brother, the count of Provence, prisoner through treachery. He immediately gathered together the barons of Provence, and they raided throughout the territory of the count of Forcalquier. The count [of Forcalquier] finally freed the count of Provence from captivity at the wish of the king. Before he left, Pedro reestablished peace and harmony between them.

When he had returned and was in the town of Montpellier, a conflict broke out between him and the men of the town.[222] An exceedingly serious scandal and estrangement arose between him and his wife on this account.[223] The king bent every effort to obtain a divorce, and Marie went to Rome to present her complaints against the king before the Supreme Pontiff. He finally decreed that there were no grounds for a divorce between them. On the contrary, in order to strengthen the marriage contracted between them, he confirmed it by papal order.[224]

The queen then rendered up her spirit to the Creator with the greatest devotion and humility. She was buried with honor in the church of Saint Peter, near the altar of Saint Petronilla. God showed the queen many favors for her merits, for, during her life and after her death, God performed many miracles through Marie.[225]

King Pedro established a close friendship with King Alfonso of Castile [VIII, 1158–1214]. When Alfonso had been defeated by the Saracens in the battle of Los Arcos, in which about forty thousand Christians were killed,[226] his uncle, King Fernando of Leon, and King Sancho of Navarre invaded the kingdom of Castile, causing great damage. King Alfonso then asked his friend, King Pedro, to come to his aid, saying that otherwise his kingdom would be exposed to ruin. King Pedro marched to his aid with a mighty army, and both together invaded and devastated the kingdom of Leon. They recovered all that Alfonso had lost.

They then invaded Navarre and took all of Guipúzcoa, Alava, and Vitoria, as well as another great territory. Pedro attacked the king of Navarre with such force that he abandoned his kingdom and fled beyond the sea.

In the course of time, the king of Aragon wished for friendship among these rulers, and returned to the king of Navarre whatever he had occupied of his realm.[227] The king of Castile, however, retained under his power that which he had occupied, and retains it still today.

Pedro, with King Alfonso, was victorious in a great battle against the Saracens at Ubeda, in which he was the outstanding warrior, with an endless eagerness to overcome the Saracens. García, bishop of Zaragoza; Berenguer, bishop-elect in Barcelona; and the nobles and knights García Romeo, Jimeno Cornel, Miguel of Luesia, Aznar Pardo, Guillem of Cervera, the count of Ampurias, Ramón Folch, and Guillem of Cardona were with Pedro at this battle. The first man to gain the wall of Ubeda was a shield-bearer by the name of Lope Ferrench of Luna. The king then returned home with honor and a famous victory.[228] He quickly seized from the Saracens the castles of Castelfabib and Ademuz, the castle of Calatrava, and many other castles which he joined to his realm.

When this campaign was over, on Monday, 17 July in the Year of Our Lord 1212, Pedro marched with all his knights and infantry beyond the pass of Muradal to a place called Las Navas de Tolosa, where he defeated King Miramamolin and his men, whom he pursued for the entire day, slaughtering a countless number of Saracens.[229] After he had gained such a great victory, and had rendered thanks to God for it, he returned home with honor.

At that time, the count of Urgell was Guiraut of Cabrera, to whom the county had passed by succession from his uncle Ermengol, who had died without children.[230] Count Guiraut waged great wars against the king and inflicted many injuries upon him. The king, in response, besieged the city of Balaguer and the castle of Llorens, where the count was staying, with a large army. Being besieged, the count at length surrendered himself, and his wife and children, to the king, who held them prisoner in the castle of Loarre in Aragon. He kept the county of Urgell under his authority while he lived. When he died, the nobles of Catalunya took Guiraut, and his wife and children, from the procurators of the kingdom of Aragon. When he had been delivered from captivity, Guiraut immediately gave himself up to the Knights Templar, where he ended his days.

In King Pedro's time, Archbishop Arnau of Narbonne, together with many men of France signed with the Cross, rose up against the heretics living in the province of Narbonne. The king, at the behest of his lord the Pope, gave the lands of Béziers and Carcassone and all their domains in fief to Simon, count of Montfort, who rendered homage to him for them, and swore fidelity to him as a vassal to his lord.

Simon attempted to disinherit the king's sisters, the countesses of Toulouse, and the king warned and requested him to avoid causing his sisters any injury or damage. When Simon, arrogant in his obstinacy and obstinate in his arrogance, treated these warnings and pleas with contempt, the king sent envoys to the Supreme Pontiff to beg him to deign to write Simon that he should not disinherit the suppliant sisters. Simon was nevertheless unwilling to restrain himself from this enterprise. For this reason, and impatient of these damages and injuries, the king and a massive army marched to the aid of the count of Toulouse, with whom the count of Foix and many other barons were allied. Once united, they attacked the count of Montfort, and put him to flight so swiftly that they forced him to take refuge in the castle of Muret. The king and the counts of Foix and Toulouse joined here to do battle against Simon. The counts of Foix and Toulouse, however, fled and abandoned King Pedro in the midst of battle. Since the king had never turned his back to the enemy, he decided that it was better to die with honor than to live like a fugitive in dishonor and disgrace. Another chronicle, however, states that his brother-in-law Raymond, count of Toulouse, directed to the king a plea that he should come to his assistance because he was at war with the king of France.[231]

Since Count Raymond of Toulouse was protecting some heretics, Archbishop Arnau of Narbonne arranged that, after Raymond's death, the king of Aragon should take his daughter in marriage and that the county of Toulouse should remain under the House of Aragon.[232]

The king of Aragon mortgaged many villages for this reason and seized the tithes of his lands and wealth from the treasuries of churches. For this reason, it is believed, the wrath of God descended upon him, and he marched through the pass of Muradal.[233]

Simon of Montfort, who was waging war for the king of France, shut himself and his men up in the castle of Muret, which the king of Aragon, in company with the count of Foix and certain other counts of Gascony, then besieged. Simon offered to surrender himself to the king according to the good customs of France, but the king refused to accept.[234] Seeing themselves facing death, the French made a sudden dawn attack from the castle. Not shunning all the troubles their foes had avoided,[235] they reached the king and killed him and others named above, along with many barons of Aragon. Among the latter were Aznar Pardo, his son Pedro Pardo, Gómez of Luna, Miguel of Luesia, and many others of Aragon. No one from Catalunya perished.[236]

The king died in his sixtieth year of age and of that of the Lord the 1214th.[237] He reigned for seventeen years, four months, and eighteen days.

He was buried in the monastery of Sigena, which his mother Sancha had built and established as a convent for the women of the Order of the Hospital of Jerusalem.[238]

This king went to the lands of Toulouse only for the purpose of giving aid to his sisters, as was stated above, and not to help any infidels or enemies of the orthodox faith, of which he was a member and in which he persisted faithfully and without blemish all his life.

Chapter 35

KING JAIME [I, 1213–1276] AND HIS DEEDS, AND THE CAPTURE OF MALLORCA AND VALENCIA[239]

King Pedro was survived by a son named Jaime, surnamed "the Fortunate."[240] He was called "the Fortunate" because, since ancient times, no one had achieved so many and such great victories with so few battles.

Jaime was given to the count of Montfort to be reared. Simon was supposed to give Jaime his daughter as wife, together with all the land that he had acquired after the death of King Pedro.[241] Because Count Simon had been the cause of the death of King Pedro, Jaime's father, however, the pope ordered that Jaime be returned to his own people.

There was much conflict among the people of Aragon over the choice of a king. Some, and with them the greater part of the nobility of Aragon, wanted Fernando, abbot of the monastery of Montearagón and brother of King Pedro, to be king. Although he might have been an abbot, he behaved like a knight and appropriated the renders of the monastery.[242] Pedro Fernández of Azagra, lord of Albarracín, opposed this selection, and the populace of the entire kingdom wished to see Jaime's birthright protected, since rule of the kingdom was due him by hereditary succession.

Because of this division of opinion, the Lord Supreme Pontiff sent a cardinal named Peter of Benevento to the count of Montfort. He took Jaime and restored him to his subjects.[243] Bishop Ispan of Segovia and the lord of Albarracín arranged this matter at their own expense.

When the cardinal had brought Jaime into his own lands, he had all the barons and nobles of the country gather in the castle of Monzón and, in their presence, commended Jaime to be reared by his uncle Sanç.[244] There was great discord among the barons, burgesses, and men of the towns because Jaime was without natural authority or discretion due to his tender age. The cardinal quelled this dissension, desiring peace and concord among all groups. He worked so hard and effectively that the barons and others swore fidelity as vassals to Jaime as their natural lord. Intervening in the matter with the general consent of all involved, he established and ordained three procurators in Jaime's jurisdiction: one in Catalunya and two in Aragon, one from the mountains to the Ebro and the other from the Ebro up to Castile. Jaime's uncle, Count Sanç of Rosselló, would direct the procurators and govern Jaime's places and lands as general procurator. He was to rule and govern faithfully, and to continue to do so until Jaime reached the age when he knew how to govern his lands himself.[245]

When Jaime reached this age, a solemn festival was celebrated in the city of Tarazona, he received the order of knighthood, and was raised up as king.[246]

Those who were opposed to him and wished to rebel immediately took to flight. They went to the city of Teruel, and the king pursued them there. Some fled to parts of Castile and others to the city of Valencia, which was in Saracen hands at the time. The king later forgave them and they returned home.[247]

After this, at the instigation of certain people, the procurators and governors of the king were accused in his presence. Pedro Ahones was killed on this account, and the others were held in disfavor. For this reason, the following verse was pertinent: "He who serves a child gains nothing, loses everything."[248]

Jaime married Eleanora, daughter of the king of Castile, from whom he had a son called Alfonso.[249] Because the couple were found to be in a degree of consanguinity so close that their marriage could not be tolerated without sin, however, John, cardinal-bishop of Santa Sabina, separated them.[250] Alfonso, their son, died without issue and was buried in the monastery of Veruela.

Jaime then married the daughter of the king of Hungary. She was called Andrea and was later called Violant, and was the niece of the Emperor of Constantinople.[251] He had three sons from her: Pedro, Jaime, and Sancho, who was the archbishop of Toledo. Archbishop Sancho went to Spain against the Saracens to spread the True Faith and exalt the Divine Name. After many victories over the Saracens in the service of God, he closed his last day—the manner of his death is uncertain—in the Moroccan [*sic*] city of Jaén.[252]

The king had four daughters from his wife, of whom one was called Violante. She was the wife of Alfonso,[253] first-born of the king of Castile, who was elected Emperor of Germany, but did not obtain that dignity for certain reasons. The second daughter was Constanza, who was the wife of Manuel, brother of King Alfonso of Castile. The third was Isabel, the wife of Philip, first-born of King Louis of France. The fourth was Maria, who did not marry.

The king had other sons and daughters besides these. By the noble Teresa Gil of Bidaura, he fathered Jaime of Exerica and Pedro of Ayerbe, who were both legitimate, a fact that their mother managed to prove, but not without great difficulty. From other noble ladies, he fathered Fernando Sánchez of Castro and Pedro Fernández of Ixer.

In King Jaime's days, Pons of Cabrera [1231–1243], son of Guiraut of Cabrera, was the count of Urgell. Pons died in the Year of Our Lord 1243. His son Alvaro, sometimes known as Ermengol, was count after him [Ermengol IX, 1243–1256]. Count Alvaro had two wives, one of whom was the daughter of Pere of Moncada, from whom he had a daughter whom he gave as wife to Sancho of Antillon. The other was the sister of Count Roger of Foix, called Cecilia, from whom he had two sons, Ermengol and Alvaro. Count Alvaro was a noble man, generous, able, diligent, and ingenious, but because of the discord between him and his first wife and because he abandoned her, he endured many labors and troubles. Count Ermengol died in the Year of Our Lord 1247 and left his county in great dissension and tribulation. Indeed, King Jaime took it into his own hands. He had previously acquired the county in the time of the above-mentioned Count Ermengol of Urgell, through Aurembaix, daughter of the above-mentioned Ermengol, count of Urgell. But, as a special favor, he had restored the county to Ermengol, son of the Alvaro who married the daughter of Pere of Moncada. He gave the viscounties of Ager and Castellon to Ermengol's brother, Alvarono, who married the daughter of Ramón of Cardona.

The count of Ampurias at the time was Huc [III, 1160–1230], a most noble man who ruled his county prudently and was present with King Jaime at the capture of Mallorca, where he died like a brave knight. He was succeeded by Pons Huc [II, 1230–1267], who was a very willing and prudent knight, and a victor over his foes. He had many conflicts with Jaufre, viscount of Rocabertí, and with Oliver of Terme. One day, Oliver invaded Ampurias with a hundred cavalry and many infantry, intending to devastate the county. The count of Ampurias gathered his vassals, pursued Oliver, and besieged him in the place of Armentera. He did not withdraw until he captured Oliver and all of his warriors. Huc was later present, with fifty cavalry maintained at his own expense, in aid of King Jaime at the capture of Valencia.

The worthy King Jaime, wishing to emulate his predecessors, began to wage war against the Saracens. In order to announce his intention of destroying the Saracen nation and converting it to the faith of the Cross, and wishing to make his name familiar to all, he convened a general assembly to which the archbishops, bishops, prelates, barons, the mayors of the cities and towns, and many other people came. It was agreed here that King Jaime should go to the kingdom of Mallorca, and wrest it from the hands of the Saracens.[254]

The necessary fleet was prepared without delay, and he sailed with fighting men of Catalunya and Aragon, both cavalry and infantry. He besieged the city of Mallorca, which, after some time, with the help of God and the force of arms, he captured on the feast of Saint Sylvester [31 December] in the Year of Our Lord 1229. Countless Saracens died here; some were killed, others became captives, and none escaped.

When this most powerful king entered the city, he found the king of the Saracens trapped in a dead-end street, and seized him by the beard.[255]

He then subjugated the island of Mallorca and the island of Menorca to the payment of tribute to him.[256] When the necessary garrison had been placed in the city and island of Mallorca, the cathedral church established, and others built there in honor of God, Jaime rendered thanks to Him and His Glorious Mother for such a celebrated victory, and joyfully returned to Catalunya.

After several days, growing impatient of quiet, having held a conference with his subjects, he laid siege to the city of Valencia with many cavalry and infantry.[257] After a long siege and the pressure of major and lesser assaults, it surrendered to the king on the feast of Saint Michael [29 September] in the Year of Our Lord 1238. He then subjugated the entire kingdom of Valencia, not without laborious difficulty, to his authority. He quickly built a cathedral church and many other churches in that city and kingdom, rendering praise and glory to the Highest and to the Blessed Virgin Mary for such great and special favors shown to him. By reason of these favors and victories, his soul conceived a deep affection for this city, and he proposed with all his will to persist diligently in the destruction of the lands and kingdoms of the Saracens.

Therefore, after the counsel and mature deliberation of his noble vassals, he went with a great multitude of knights and soldiers to besiege the city of Murcia, which had not yet fallen to him by conquest or subjugation, and decisively overcame it and all its realm. Rendering thanks as above, he built in that city and realm a cathedral church and many other churches in praise and glory of the Divine Name.[258]

Immediately after he had conquered the city and realm of Murcia, he turned it over to the king of Castile, establishing it as the dowry of his daughter Violant, whom he gave in marriage to Prince Alfonso, eldest son of the king of Castile. He did this because its conquest and subjugation belonged to the king of Castile by apostolic concession.[259] Indeed, Prince Alfonso had besieged the city of Murcia for a long time, but, when he was not able to capture it, he retired upon the advice of his vassals. After his departure, King Jaime besieged and took it.

The worthy King Jaime was an excellent ruler, vigorous, charming, kindly, pious, and a marvelous warrior, father of orphans, defender of widows, and provider for disinherited barons, to whom he gave towns, castles, and lands with which they might honorably maintain their stations.

He gave the prince of Portugal, who was an exile from his land, the island of Mallorca for his lifetime.[260] With the aid of the bishop of Tarragona, the prince seized the island of Ibiza from the Saracens. Jaime gave the distinguished exiled knight Bretó of Marseilles the castle of San Lorenzo and the castle of Tagello. He showed similar favor to several others who could not be encompassed in a short discussion.

Beyond this, this virtuous king built two thousand churches for the exaltation of the Divine Name in the lands that he had seized from the Saracens. He built many monasteries, of various orders, such as the monastery of Benifazá, which is in the kingdom of Valencia, in which he placed monks of the monastery of Poblet. He built all the monasteries of the Friars Preacher and Minor of all his realms, of which he placed the first stones of the foundations with his own hands, praising God and giving from his treasury for their construction. Wherever he happened to be, he provided food for all orders of religious men.

Justice concurred with mercy in him, for whenever he condemned anyone to death, he would be moved by pity and would burst into tears. But his mercy never impaired his sense of justice.

King Jaime was in the city of Lyon, by the Rhone River, and paid reverence to the lord Pope Gregory X [1271–1276], who was there because it had been decided and proclaimed at that time that the Christians should take passage to the Holy Land.[261] Although the king was then old and weighed down with years, he neither shunned bodily labors nor was he forgetful of the famous triumphs that God had conferred upon him in His service, in which he had freely spent his youth. He therefore proposed to devote whatever years remained to him in going to the Holy Land himself and ending his days there with honor.

But the expedition did not take place,[262] and he returned home. He then proclaimed that his eldest son, Pedro, should be king of Aragon and Valencia and count of Barcelona after his death, and that his second son, Jaime, should be king of the Balearics, count of Rosselló and Cerdanya, and lord of Montpellier.[263] This displeased his subjects immensely.

He was so just and reasonable that, up to then, it had been unheard of that he should do anything that his subjects would find displeasing. It once happened that, while he was lying in bed at Montpellier, confined by a serious illness, the Glorious Virgin Mother of God appeared to him with immense joy, telling him that he should arise from his bed healthy, which he did. For this miracle, he paid a great deal out of his treasury to build the church of Vallverde in honor of the Virgin Mary.[264]

Many of the saints aided him and his subjects fighting for him when he struggled against the Saracens. Once, he sent the noble knight Bernat Guillem of Entença with other knights of Catalunya and Aragon into Valencia. They were on a certain hill now called Santa María del Puig and a countless number of Saracens had rushed upon them. When the battle raged most fiercely between them, Saint George appeared with a great army of celestial knights. With their aid, the Christians gained the day without a single one of them dying in battle.

This excellent king was very reverent toward God, the Blessed Mary, and all the saints. Among other devout words, he said these: "Lord, Almighty God, make me despise the fortunes of this world and not fear adversity. O Lord, let You Yourself be the Defender and Guardian of the people which You have committed to my rule. God, reach out quickly in my aid, in aid of my weakness" (Psalms 69:2). "Glory be to the Father, and to the Son, and to the Holy Spirit." "Teach me, my Lord, to do Your will, because You are my God, and it pleases You, O Lord, that I should be Your servant" (Psalms 142:10). "Aid us, God of our salvation, and turn Your anger from us" (Psalms 78:9). For these prayers and his other merits, God caused him to live a long time in His service.

At the end of his life, this virtuous king was admitted into the rule of the monastery of Poblet, of the Cistercian order, and received the monastic habit.[265]

Before he took the monk's habit, he called his son Pedro to the village of Alcira, where he lay ill, and said to him, "My son, know that I am going to God, my Creator, and that I shall be forgiven because of His mercy. Therefore, I give to you the realms which He commended to me and which I ruled with His grace and mercy. I beg and admonish you, my son, by the bowels of the mercy of God and of our Lord Jesus Christ, let there be compassion and justice in you, and may you therefore love and cherish your subjects, because where there is love and charity there truly is God. Wherefore I beseech you, my son, that these things may be in you always, and that God may be with you, and that you may live always with Him, my son. I give you my sword as a sign of justice and righteousness, with which you may separate the bad from the good. And I give you my dominion, and with it may God give you victory over your foes. I entreat you, my son, to love your barons, knights, and faithful subjects, who loved me with all their hearts, and who risked their hearts and properties and bodies in my service and that of God. At your elevation, be as compassionate with them as may be needed, so that God may be compassionate with you. Love them so that they may love you; amplify your patience and humility, which are the foundations of all good things. I beg you, my son, that you may love your brother, who is wise, good, and of an honest life, lest any of those things which I gave to him should arouse envy in you. And I command both of you to love each other invincibly, as I have loved you."266

Having said this, the pious king commanded them to bring him the wood of the True and Holy Cross of Jesus Christ which he possessed. Holding it, he said, "My most beloved son, I commend myself to God, Who is calling me to His Glory. May the Father, Son, and Holy Spirit bless you. I ask the mercy of God, that He may cause you to reign long, according to His justice and holy mercy."

After this, the king humbly shed his royal robes, praising God and loudly singing the hymn, "Veni, Creator Spiritus." He donned the habit of the monks of the monastery of Poblet, who were there present. Then, with great devotion and humility, he received the Body of Our Lord. He then asked and commanded his son Pedro to keep in his heart the execution of all those things which he had set forth in his testament or otherwise, in reverence of God and for the remission of his sins.267

When the supreme moment of his life drew near, he lifted his eyes toward heaven, to God the Father Almighty, and tearfully said, "O Lord God, I shall enter into Your house and I shall worship toward Your holy temple" (Psalms 5:8), "And I shall confess Your Name, O Lord" (Psalms 85:12), "In Your hands I commend my spirit" (Psalms 30:6), "You have redeemed me, O Lord God of Truth" (Psalms 30:6), "O Lord God, You are the Power, You are the Kingdom, and You, O Lord, are above all kings, and all things are under Your sway. O Lord, I accepted from You a kingdom which I returned to You. May it please You, O Lord, to gather my soul into the eternal light of Your presence."

Calling upon divine mercy, he then gave up his spirit. His body was placed with pomp and honor in a sepulcher near the altar of the Blessed Mary in the cathedral of Valencia. Later, in accordance with the profession of his vows, it was removed to the monastery of Poblet. This blessed king completed the course of his present life happily in the seventy-second year of his life, on the twenty-seventh day of July in the Year of Our Lord 1276. He ruled sixty-two years, eleven months, nine days.

For a year before the death of the king, which could be seen to be drawing near, and no less afterward, all Spain gave way to great groans and tears, and not without reason. For countless Saracen peoples [the Almohades], knowing that the hour of the death of that glorious king was drawing near, rushed into Spain. They killed a particularly noble man, Sancho, archbishop of Toledo and son of King Jaime, and Nuño, a noble baron of Castile, and many other barons and nobles.[268] They then occupied many castles and places in Spain and caused so much destruction that it is impossible to recount it.

Chapter 36
KING PEDRO THE GREAT [III, 1276–1285] AND HIS DEEDS[269]

King Jaime's son, Pedro, surnamed "the Great," succeeded him in the kingdoms of Aragon and Valencia and in the county of Barcelona. He was called "the Great" because he fought numerous great battles against many Christian and Saracen kings, as well as against the Church, all at the same time. In the kingdom of Mallorca, the counties of Rosselló and Cerdanya, and in the barony of Montpellier, Jaime was succeeded by his son, Jaime. Unmindful of his father's advice, he was extremely disobedient to his brother Pedro, as we shall further disclose below.

Pedro, of noble birth and refusing to be unworthy of his ancestors, gallantly and constantly planned in his heart to attack the evil of the Saracens, over whom, as over his other enemies, he always achieved victory.

But he first decided to besiege and capture the fortress of Hostales, because of the many labors and injuries that Guillem Galceran, lord of Hostales, had caused his father, King Jaime.

And because of the various injuries and damage that Guillem Ramón of Odena had committed and occasioned King Jaime and his subjects over time and contrary to the law, Pedro drowned him in the sea.

When King Jaime was still alive, he held the city of Murcia under a strict siege. Through the many skirmishes and the assaults of the siege machinery participating in this operation, and because of the vigilant care, prudent counsel, and discipline of the warriors of King Pedro, at that time still a prince, the inhabitants of the city were exposed to hunger and many other ills. Bypassing King Jaime, they wished to surrender themselves to the said prince, but he did not want this. Preferring to defer to his father, he arranged that they should surrender themselves to him.[270]

King Jaime fathered many children, both from noble ladies as well as from others, whom we do not mention because they were not descended from a legitimate line. Nevertheless, there was one, named Fernando Sánchez, in whom the wealth and power he possessed engendered arrogance. He accused and defamed his brother King Pedro, then a prince, in many ways before their father. For this reason, the father came to consider Pedro dangerous to have in the house. Not content with this, Fernando hatched many plots with knights and burgesses of Aragon and Catalunya, and with King Charles of Sicily, against his brother. King Pedro waged war against Fernando on this account, confiscated his lands, and finally, having captured him near the castle of Pomar, had him drowned in the river Cinca for the wrongs he had worked against him.

Even after the conquest of the kingdom of Valencia from the Saracens by his father, many Saracens still remained, holding fortresses there. After some time, they rebelled against King Jaime, capturing and killing many Christians of that realm. At length, a large number of Christians went out to quell the rebellion. Brother Pedro of Moncayo, Master of the Order of the Knights of the Temple in Spain, was captured in an engagement with the Saracens, and many brother knights of the order were killed. The master escaped his captivity, however, by fleeing with his bodyguard.[271]

The enemies of the Catholic faith did inestimable damage to the kingdom of Valencia and to the Church of God. A Saracen named al-Azraq was their leader, and all of the Saracens followed him. King Pedro killed him and his followers; they had clearly placed not only this kingdom, but the whole of Spain, in danger, and exposed the Catholic faith to injury.

In King Jaime's old age, he was worn out by a constant fever and unable to resist the Saracens. King Pedro, then still a prince, knowing that the kingdom was exposed to ruin, faced the Saracens himself, like a bulwark of the True Faith. Wishing to emulate his father in such deeds, he wrested the previously mentioned fortresses from the Saracens and, with the great-est valor, ousted them from the entire kingdom of Valencia. Because of King Pedro's energetic forcefulness, the kingdom thus stood in tranquility and serenity, and the storm of war was transformed into the calm of peace. His subjects could truly say that to a good father a not lesser son had succeeded in realms and in lands.

After a time, King Pedro, with a large force of knights and infantry of his kingdom, besieged a castle called Montesa. It was marvelously well fortified, and had not been captured during the conquest of the kingdom of Valencia. Although the Saracens had held it since ancient times, Pedro bravely attacked it. With the aid of God, he took it and led to Christianity the enemies of the Cross driven from that place.[272]

Having accomplished these things, the king was unwilling that his beloved father should be forgotten, but that rather we should comply with his requests. Accompanied by a great assembly of archbishops, bishops, prelates, and other noble persons, he carried his father's body in his own arms to be entombed in the monastery of Poblet, where a monument of marvelous design had been constructed.

When this had been done, the king ordered a general assembly to convene at the city of Zaragoza, at which his brother Jaime, king of Mallorca, was present. Pedro was there crowned and anointed in his king-dom with honor and renowned solemnity.[273] After some time had passed, he went to Perpignan, and, at his request, his brother, King Jaime of Mallorca, offered Pedro homage and an oath of fidelity for the lands he held of him, and Pedro had his subjects and vassals do the same.[274]

Later, King Alfonso of Castile treated his wife, King Pedro's sister, wrongfully and without the marital love and honor in which she should have been held. Mistrust arose on both sides, and Pedro entered Castile under arms for six days. He led away with him his sister and her children, as well as Fernando, the first-born son of the king of Castile, whom he safeguarded in his own kingdom.[275] After some time, he restored the queen and his son to Alfonso, king of Castile, for he had not taken them away with him to keep them.

After this, there was discord and war between King Pedro and the counts of Urgell and Foix concerning the jurisdiction and other rights King Pedro declared himself to hold over the county of Urgell.[276] He besieged the castle of Pons and destroyed its village. He finally took the castle and captured the count of Urgell, Guillem of Pons, and certain knights of the count of Foix. He freed them from prison after a time and, by his grace, restored the county to the count of Urgell, who rendered that which was proper to the king.

Then, because of certain questions that the king raised against the nobles of Catalunya, the greater part of them, together with the counts of Urgell and Foix, waged war against the king and gathered in the castle of Balaguer to coordinate their plans against him.[277] Learning of their little assembly, he marched day and night toward the castle of Balaguer with men of the cities and towns of Catalunya, and placed it under a powerful and close siege. By the strictness of his siege, he kept the nobles and barons who were shut up in that castle suffering from lack of food and other necessities. They were not able to supply themselves because of the rigorous blockade. They therefore placed themselves and their lands unconditionally in the king's hands. The nobles Roger Bernard, count of Foix; Ermengol, count of Urgell; his brother Alvaro, viscount of Ager; his brother Ramón Roger, count of Pallars; Ramón Folch, viscount of Cardona; Ramón, viscount of Villamur; Pons of Ribellas; Ramón of Anglesola; and many other nobles and knights had all been in the castle of Balaguer.[278]

The count of Urgell was placed in the prison of the castle of Ciurana under heavy chains, and the other nobles and knights were detained, as prisoners in shackles and fetters, in various fortresses and places of the realm. After the passage of some time, however, he freed them all from prison and graciously restored them to their own lands.

King Pedro, thereby being at peace and harmony with all those of Catalunya, wished to have a meeting and conference with the king of France. Gathering a large and distinguished army of his subjects, he met with his brother-in-law, Philip, king of France [III, 1271–1285]. After they had had a long discussion, King Pedro most urgently asked Philip for the viscounty of Fenollades, the counties of Carcassone, Gavaldan, Milhau, and Béziers, and certain other lands. He also asked the king for all the rights due from his brother, King Jaime of Mallorca, by reason of the lordship of Montpellier and other lands he possessed appurtenant to the county of Barcelona. But the king of France was not willing to grant him any of these requests and immediately returned to his own land.[279]

Wishing to follow in the praiseworthy footsteps of his predecessors, Pedro prepared a great war fleet manned by many cavalry and infantry of his land prepared for war.[280] He boarded his fleet at Portfangós and sailed to Barbary.[281] He landed at a fortress called Alcoyll,[282] and seized it and many nearby places. He waged battles against the Saracens, over whom he always triumphed. He built a church in this castle and placed it under the invocation of Saint Peter, because it was on the vigil of Saint Peter's day [28 June] that he had arrived at the fortress of Alcoyll.

Occupying the captured fortress with joy and delight, King Pedro then sent solemn emissaries to the lord Pope Martin [IV, 1281–1285], asking that, since he intended to subjugate Africa and spread the name of the Lord and the Christian faith in it, the pope should now deign to grant indulgences to those who were present with him as well as to those who were to come. He additionally asked the pope to provide him with aid and assistance. The pope, however, led by less able counsel, did not receive these emissaries with the kindness he should have shown, but brusquely denied them everything they asked.[283] When they had returned empty-handed to the king, they informed him how badly and how hatefully the pope had acted toward them personally and in the audience they had had. This made the king very sad at heart.

A few days later, emissaries to the king arrived from Sicily. In a long presentation, they related to him how Conrad, king of Sicily, had been defeated and captured by King Charles [of Anjou, 1266–1282], and savagely beheaded at Salerno;[284] how King Charles was destroying and unjustly occupying Sicily, which pertained by right to the same Pedro;[285] how he was afflicting the nobles and even the common people of Sicily with many and most cruel kinds of executions; how the French were incessantly visiting hateful and disgraceful injuries upon the Sicilians, deflowering virgins, violently seizing widows and the Sicilians' wives,[286] and inflicting upon them other evils impossible to unfold. Therefore, groaning, lamenting, and loosing sobs from their breasts, they were asking God and King Pedro, after God their only refuge, to whom the succession to the kingdom of Sicily belonged, that he should deign to liberate them from so many tribulations.

Considering the desolation and misery by which the Sicilians were being oppressed, and remembering the Supreme Pontiff's denial of the indulgences and assistance requested of him, the king decided to alter the laudable project he had conceived of attacking the enemies of the Christian faith into one of attacking the many calamities and miseries that were destroying the Sicilians.

He immediately ordered the emissaries to return home and commanded the Sicilians to show no service to King Charles, but rather to incite rebellion and rise up against him since he was the unjust occupier of their lands. He promised to be with them shortly, God willing. The emissaries were overjoyed by this and returned to Sicily. The Sicilians immediately rose in rebellion against King Charles, who had assembled a large army against the emperor of Constantinople and was then besieging the city of Messina.

Having compassion on the Sicilians, King Pedro, with his entire fleet, withdrew from Barbary, to the rejoicing of the Saracens, who had considered themselves lost. The king and his men soon landed at the city of Trapani, which was gladdened with great joy at their arrival.[287] Among the other honors shown them was that, from the seashore where they had landed up to the city of Palermo and through the neighborhoods of the entire city, they marched along on cloths of gold and silk.[288] Pedro left Palermo without delay and marched toward the city of Messina, to the defense of which he had already sent a company of infantry, and he was received there with joy by the crowd.[289] King Charles, learning that King Pedro had entered Messina and had taken it under his dominion, lifted his siege. The greatest concern of the French was to board the fleet that Charles had there and to escape the hands of King Pedro.

While the French were fleeing toward the sea, King Pedro and his men went after them like a bolt of lighting, charged, and struck.[290] Many died in this blow, and the attackers seized vessels, laden with food and other spoils, which had been unable to join the French fleet.

When King Charles had been thus defeated and expelled from the kingdom of Sicily, and all the realm had been subjected to the dominion of King Pedro, he confirmed to the nobles and knights of the cities and villages their privileges, liberties, and immunities; and he did and granted many good things for the common people. He then ordered his wife Constanza to come to Sicily with their children, which she did, and great honor was shown to her, as their queen and mistress, by the Sicilians. The first of her children was called Alfonso, the second Jaime, the third Federico, and the fourth Pedro.

When King Charles was in Calabria, and he and his men were sunk in hatred and melancholy, they plotted many things against the king their conqueror. Wishing to expel King Charles with his forces and adherents from Calabria, King Pedro sent many battle-hardened knights and infantry there, men neither weakened by winter nor slowed by heat, to whom the use of arms was not at all laborious.[291] These forces conquered a large part of Calabria and, in numerous battles against King Charles, always triumphed. In one such battle, the count of Lenzo, brother of the king of France, was killed.

With these sorts of things being practiced by each king against the other, violation of faith became a cause of mutual misfortune and a further provocation for war. Under the influence of the king of England,[292] the constant fighting was ended, and both kings agreed to a personal battle in the field, each with a hundred knights. The condition and agreement was added that whoever obtained victory in this battle would be king of Sicily absolutely and without any contrary claim; and that the other would never entitle himself king. The day and place for the staging of the battle was scheduled by them for Bordeaux, which is in the jurisdiction of the king of England.[293]

Because of this commitment, and so that the kingdom of Sicily might be kept more secure and uninjured by the insults of its enemies, King Pedro built many war galleys. He appointed a noble Sicilian named Roger de Lauria, who had been educated in the king's court for a long time, admiral over this fleet. The king then returned to Catalunya secretly, with victory and honor.[294]

As the day agreed upon for the battle approached, the king made no preparation for going to it; this was because the field chosen for the battle was inconvenient and suspicious to him for many reasons. His opponents therefore believed him to be prostrate with fear and not daring to enter into battle against them. As the day for the battle drew near, the king most secretly took as his companion Jaime de Figuera of Calatayud, a horse dealer who was well known in those parts, and, in the clothes of a merchant and with a merchant's bag, went riding swiftly to Bordeaux, where the combat was to be held. And it was then the day agreed upon for the battle.

King Charles was encamped near Bordeaux with his brother, the king of France, and a great force of armed supporters. They intended to do battle with a hundred knights, as was agreed, and to capture or kill King Pedro.

Pedro was then entering the lists armed beautifully and as was fitting when entering the field of combat. The seneschal of Bordeaux and many people of the city were there. Raising his voice, King Pedro called to him, "Seneschal, I am Pedro of Aragon, who has come upon this agreed day for the purpose of matching myself in battle in your presence, or in that of him who in the place of the king of England is supposed to keep the field secure. Is it in your power to do so?" The seneschal answered him, "I am not able to keep the field safe for you; neither could the king of England himself do so if he were here. And, since no one of the opposing party is here, I command you on behalf of the king of England to leave the field."[295] The king requested that he have a public document drawn up to that effect. He then rode his horse swiftly around the edge of the field, shouting in a loud voice. "Is King Charles, or anyone standing in for him, here? I am the king of Aragon, prepared to do and undergo that which is proper in trial by combat." He repeatedly offered these and other words in ratification of his right, requiring a notary who was there to draw up a legal document recording his readiness to enter combat and the forswearing and contumacy of King Charles, as a permanent record of these matters. Immediately seizing the document, and riding swiftly through day and night, he returned to his own country.[296]

Meanwhile, Admiral Roger de Lauria, who had remained in Sicily with King Pedro's children, went to the city of Naples with an armed fleet to provoke and injure Pedro's enemies. Prince Charles of Salerno, eldest son of King Charles, was then near the city with many nobles, knights, and picked men-at-arms of Naples. He boarded his galleys with great pomp and fiercely attacked Roger's fleet. After a most bitter conflict, Roger gained the upper hand and carried off Charles and all his galleys, of which none escaped. He took all the booty to Sicily with the greatest delight, and turned Charles and all his nobles over to Jaime, son of Pedro. Pedro and his subjects were filled with merriment when this news arrived.

As for other matters, when some time had passed, Juan Nuñez, baron of the kingdom of Castile and lord of the castle of Albarracín, denied this castle to King Pedro. Because of this and several other injuries he had caused the king and his subjects, Pedro besieged his castle. The kings of France and Castile made veiled threats to Pedro that he should desist from the siege. He refused to do so, however, and at length took the castle.[297]

While engaged in the siege, he learned that King Charles had left this world, which he did not wish to tell anyone. Indeed he said that one of the best knights in the world had died.[298]

After this, the king of France sent the seneschal of Toulouse with Juan Nuñez of Lara, and they seized Aragon. King Pedro went to Tarazona to do battle with them.[299] Not having expected this, they fled to the kingdom of Navarre, which was aiding the king of France. They then invaded Aragon by way of Valdonsella. The place of Ull was a tower, the castellan of which was named Jiménez of Artieda. Although it was not very strong, he nevertheless made a valiant effort to defend it as if it in fact were, because he was unwilling to surrender it. Digging away at its base, the French destroyed half of the tower, and the castellan remained in the other half, now with neither weapons nor food. Nevertheless, he decided that it would be a better thing to perish in that tower than to abandon it. When the enemy scaled the part of the tower that was still standing, he hurled his helmet and other armor at those who were climbing up. And he hit them.

The French did not wish to kill him, since their captain had commanded that a man so exemplary in loyalty and faithfulness should not die. They therefore took him prisoner and carried him back to France. He was released from prison after a time, but he did not venture to return to Aragon, since he was ashamed of having lost the tower under his command. This caused Pedro to feel ashamed also, because he had not been able to go to his castellan's aid.

Having destroyed these two places, the enemy, with the help of certain knights of that region who were of the blood of the Sarassa of Navarre, marched through the valley of Pintano, reaching Bailó and Arbués, which they burned. Entering the valley of the Aragón, they came to the town of Berdún and destroyed it by fire. They then seized Salvatierra and built a fine castle there, which still stands. The French held it until peace was made between the kings of France and Aragon. Bertrand of Ile held it for the king of France.

King Pedro was in a state of perplexity in these times, and one of his knights, named Pedro Martínez of Bolea, wished to serve the king and the kingdom. He asked King Pedro to give him credentials to the king of Castile, who had now invaded Aragon. Since the French had just invaded Catalunya, the king agreed.

This knight approached the king of Castile with these credentials and presented matters to him in the following fashion: that the king of Aragon wished to give Calatayud with all its appurtenances to him, and that in exchange the king of Castile should not make war against him. The king of Castile agreed to this. Returning to the king of Aragon, who was in Girona facing the French, he said to King Pedro that he should not worry about the king of Castile. He told him only this and nothing more, lest the king be disturbed at the concession he had made to the king of Castile.

A month passed, during which the king of Aragon achieved victory over the French. The king of Castile then requested the king of Aragon to turn Calatayud with its appurtenances over to him, as he had promised, or he would wage war against Pedro. The king was greatly astonished at this, and called Pedro Martínez of Bolea to learn from him what this might be about. The knight related the episode to the king, adding that he had gone to the court of the king of Castile. He disclosed what he had promised the king of Castile on behalf of the king of Aragon when he was at the court.

The king had known nothing of this until now, through the letter he had received from the king of Castile. Pedro Martínez declared that he had made this promise as the king's vassal and liege man lest the king should have lost his realm. The king said to him, "Do you swear that the matter was so?" "It was so," he answered, adding that the king might do whatever he pleased with him. The king, considering that Pedro Martínez had acted with good intentions to aid his king, was merciful to him. He said to him, "You are leaving in an evil hour; because of your dealings, we have lost the realm of Aragon."[300]

Also at this time, Rodrigo Vicarra, a knight and the king's captain of the kingdom of Murcia, realized that he faced pressure from all sides. He begged the king to give him credentials to the king of Granada, so that he could see if he could come to some agreement with him. Having received the letters, he quickly went to the king of Granada and presented his credentials. Studiously watching and searching out how he might be of some service to King Pedro, he told the king of Granada that he had come on behalf of the king of Aragon to denounce the treaties existing between Aragon and Granada and to defy him. The king of Granada, who had already held deliberations on these matters, told him that the troubles between the Christian kings were no reason to break off relations with him. He asked Rodrigo to arrange with the king of Aragon to extend the treaties existing between them unchanged for another five years. He would give the king sufficient money to support three hundred knights for a year, and would also reward Rodrigo. Rodrigo promised to plead on behalf of the king of Granada that King Pedro should accept these offers. The king of Granada reaffirmed his promises, and Rodrigo immediately returned to the king of Aragon with the money mentioned above. The king was very pleased, seeing the men about him so attentive of his welfare. The money was turned over to the king, who was low in funds at the time, and he ratified the treaties requested by the king of Granada.

After these events, King Pedro commanded his brother, King Jaime of Mallorca, by the bonds of his vow of homage, to which he was obligated because of the lands he held of Pedro in fief, to come to his court, because the king of France was beginning to prepare to move against King Pedro. King Jaime refused to obey his command. King Pedro therefore went to Perpignan and seized King Jaime, his wife and children, all of his counselors, and Manrique, viscount of Narbonne.

King Jaime, unwilling to be detained in prison, escaped through a sewer in the castle of Perpignan and, not without a burden of dishonor, fled. Pedro immediately led away with him the queen of Mallorca, with her children and other prisoners.[301] When they reached the town of Figueras, he turned her over to certain nobles and barons of Catalunya who were kinsmen of the queen. A knight by the name of Vilar Estarrat, however, who was an exile from the area of Carcassone and long a resident of Catalunya, secretly led away the children of the king of Mallorca and kept them in his own power. The other prisoners were not released from captivity until they had been ransomed.

Pons Huc was the count of Ampurias at that time. He had maintained an intimate friendship with King Pedro and served him whenever needed. The count carried on a long war with Pons Guillem, son of Bernat of Santa Eugenia, for the fief of the castle of Torricella, which he had refused him. When Pons Guillem tried to take the castle of Vergs by stealth, the count set a trap and caught him and many men of Torricella inside the castle. Pons Guillem and many of those with him were killed in the battle between the two forces. This Pons was killed because one day he said that he would punch the count in the jaw with his fist.

The count was a most devout Christian and reached for the divine heights. Leaving this life, he abdicated his county, giving it to his son, Huc, and entered holy orders, the order of Saint Francis to be precise. This Huc rose up against King Pedro and warred against him for the fief of Torricella. One day, the count destroyed the town of Figueras and the palace the king had built there. The king therefore assembled a number of men in the city of Girona to go out against the count. But, relying on the advice of certain barons, Huc placed himself and his lands unconditionally in the hands of the king, and humbly requested forgiveness for his deeds. The king held him captive for a few days. He then requested and commanded the count to rebuild the town of Figueras and to return whatever had been seized from there, to restore the palace there as it had been before, to take part in the work personally by carrying stones and mortar, and to level the walls of his town of Castellón d'Ampurias and of his castle of Carmenzo. Since the king had to go to Valencia, because the Saracens were vexing that kingdom, he released the count from Barcelona under parole that he would place himself in the power of the king of Aragon within thirty days.

We have discussed above how the kingdom of Sicily belonged by law to the king of Aragon and have given many other reasons why King Charles was ejected from possession of the kingdom. But because of this, Pope Martin, a native of France himself, in a full consistory to which King Pedro had not been called, pronounced sentence against him, stripping him of his realms, honors, and lands; confiscating the lands of whoever might give him aid, counsel, or favor; and placing the realm under ecclesiastical interdict. And not least, he conceded plenary remission of sins to all Christians who would go against Pedro or his lands.[302] He conceded this remission particularly to the king of France, and invested Count Charles of Valois, son of the king of France, with all of King Pedro's realms and lands.[303] Charles immediately entitled himself King of Aragon, and combined his own arms or devices with the device of the king of Aragon as if he had already gained full possession of King Pedro's lands and realms. A cardinal-legate of the Lord Pope named Carlet was selected to concede the remissions or indulgences. Because of Carlet's zeal and the indulgences, so great a multitude of people gathered against King Pedro that a great fear arose in his lands.

The king of France, with his two sons, Philip, his first-born, and Charles of Valois mentioned above, and with twenty thousand cavalry and a countless number of infantry, in the company of the aforesaid legate, arrived at Perpignan with the purpose of invading and subjugating the land of King Pedro. King Jaime of Mallorca gave his aid and favor to these enemies of King Pedro, disregarding his violation of faith and of the treaties established between him and his brother.

Hearing rumors and the tumult of the countless people who had gathered at the town of Perpignan to invade his lands, King Pedro, with the few warriors he had, went to the pass of Panissars. He took up station there to hinder the plans of the king of France and his men.[304] While King Pedro was at this pass, however, the king of France and all his men left the town of Perpignan, went to the city of Elne and attacked it fiercely. At length, and not without great effort, they took it and they put all whom they found within to a hard death. Of course, King Pedro's men caused much harm to those of their opponents who were tarrying in Rosselló. King Pedro stayed at the pass of Panissars, through which he believed that his opponents would pass. Because they feared the king, his foes avoided that road and went thorough the valley of Banyoles.[305] Behold how they employed themselves at the inception of their laudable enterprise! They looted and destroyed all the churches they encountered and committed other grave misdeeds. For this, as well as for their unjust demand that the king of Aragon be dethroned, they were exposed to suffering, grave punishments, and hardships, as we shall describe below.

When King Pedro learned that the French were passing through the valley of Banyoles, he was pained and saddened. He left the pass of Panissars and went to the town of Perelada.[306] On the advice of Dalmacio, viscount of Rocabertí, to whom the town belonged, and of other nobles and barons, he evacuated its inhabitants, put it to the torch, and destroyed it. He did this because he was not be able to defend it against the power of the French. He then went to Castellón d'Ampurias, where he stationed many knights. While Pedro tarried here, the French advanced, entering the county of Ampurias. The nobles, knights, and commoners of the county accepted the authority of the king of France, without making any distinction whatever between him and their own lord. When King Pedro learned of this, he retreated with all his troops to Girona, in order to oppose the king of the French there. The entire county of Ampurias was obeying the king of France with guile, however, so that they might be able to do him or his men injury covertly, by whatever means might become available. Wherever the French tarried, many of them perished.[307] The king of France immediately entered Castellón d'Ampurias. Because they gave themselves to him dutifully, he confirmed to the inhabitants their franchises, liberties, and privileges.

The French then went quickly to the gates of Besalú, which they found closed to them, for there were many cavalry and infantry in garrison there and in other neighboring places.

Meanwhile, many French galleys and other naval vessels landed. They were laden with food and other things necessary to the French, without which it would be impossible for them to achieve their aims. Knowing this, King Pedro expelled everyone from the city of Girona, except those required for the city's defense. He then asked Ramón Folch, viscount of Cardona, if he and a group of select knights could defend the city against the approaching enemy. This most faithful vassal undertook to do so. He selected as his lieutenants the noble Ramón of Anglesola, Guillem of Jossa, and Arnaldo of Cabrera, with many other knights who were experienced and expert at arms, and he shut himself up in the city with them.

His opponents destroyed and put to the torch all the places and fortresses that lay between Rosas and the city of Barcelona, so that he would not receive any help from the places and fortresses along the coast. Some of the galleys of the king of France were detached from the others and assigned the mission of injuring King Pedro's subjects. Ramón Marquet, a citizen of Barcelona and the king's vice-admiral, arrived in the port of Formigues with twenty galleys. There were thirty French galleys there, and he attacked them so courageously and so forcefully that he finally captured them, with a great slaughter of Frenchmen, none of whom escaped, and took them to Barcelona.

After a few days had passed, Roger de Lauria, with galleys from Sicilian waters, reached the port of Rosas, where the entire fleet of the king of France was assembled. Roger attacked fearlessly, like a bold and renowned warrior. At length, he captured the entire fleet. Many of the French who were in it were killed, and many made prisoner. He took these captives with him and sailed to Barcelona with victory and honor. Guillaume of Lodeve, admiral of the king of France, was captured in this battle, and he paid the greatest weight of gold for his ransom. The enthusiasm of the French was dampened by their opponents' victory and the loss of their fleet, and they were disinclined to continue their enterprise.[308]

The king of France reached Girona and laid siege to it.[309] There were such a great number of troops with him that they surrounded the city on all sides. They assaulted it eagerly on the vigil of Saint Peter's day [28 June], all through that night, and the following day. But those who were within inflicted such great slaughter and injuries on their attackers that they soon taught their opponents that there was little pleasure to be found in approaching the wall. But however many of the enemy were killed in the siege, such a crowd of new warriors arrived, because of the indulgences we have mentioned, that their numbers were doubled in three days.

While the city was thus under siege, the French, unrestrained by reverence for God or His saints, mutilated the body of Saint Narcissus, which was kept with the greatest veneration as a relic in the church of Saint Felix. They threw out and destroyed all the relics that were kept here and in other churches. Meanwhile, King Pedro with subtle cleverness, sometimes with ambushes and sometimes by other means, brought death and destruction to so many of the invaders that there lay a countless number of corpses all the way from the pass of Panissars down to Girona. At the same time, those in Girona made sallies against the besiegers, sometimes stealthily and sometimes openly, killing many of them and continually carrying off their horses and other equipment. King Pedro, finding it impossible to abstain from action, attacked the enemy now this way, now that. But the crowd of people who flowed in was so prodigiously great that an infinite number of them could fall without their total appearing to suffer any diminution.

A horde of Frenchmen went to the town of Banyoles to attack and destroy it. King Pedro assaulted them with the few troops he had, but so great were their numbers that the king was barely able to escape defeat.

Nevertheless, Almighty God, Whose right hand is always present in battles, did not fail to aid the king, but rather defended him from an enemy who numbered twelve thousand, and from many others advancing from the other direction. The king's companions had been delayed by a sudden emergency and were not there at the beginning of the battle, so that he was abandoned when many of his troops fled the field. Because of this, a rumor spread through the army that King Pedro had somehow fallen in combat. Those in the city of Girona were weakened and cast down by fear at this news, but their fear was turned to joy when the truth was known.[310]

After some days, the Hand of God touched the king of France mightily, so that he could not stand. This was because of the many irreverences that his men had inflicted upon Him and His saints and because of the injuries he had visited on the king of Aragon. God sent flies into his army, which was one of the plagues or curses of the pharaohs. These flies were blue on one side, and green on the other; and both sides were suffused with a bit of red. They were poisonous, so that horses and other beasts quickly died at their touch. They entered the ears and nostrils of men and beasts and did not emerge until they had brought death. The mortality from this plague in the French army grew so great that its numbers were soon diminished to a few.

Meanwhile, sickness began to break out in the city of Girona because those within were suffering from the lack of food, and also because the odor of the French corpses was pervading the city. For these reasons, and with the assent of King Pedro, Ramón Folch made an agreement with the king of France that he would surrender the city to him, and that the king of France would permit all those staying within to leave, safe and secure with all of their goods that they could carry with them. This agreement took effect on the vigil of the birth of the Blessed Mary [8 September].

The captured city was infested with flies, and their number and the pestilence caused by them were increasing daily, and the scarcity of provisions became greater. King Pedro and his men persisted in their watchful vigilance, lest food be brought in to their enemies. The king of France and his men, unable to stay any longer in this city since they could not bring in food from elsewhere, with sadness and lamenting began to withdraw. King Pedro pursued them closely and launched frequent and deadly attacks upon them. He cast down so many of them that it was marvelous and miserable to view. The king of France, so oppressed with sickness that he could not ride his horse, was carried along in his bed.[311]

When the retreating French were in the county of Ampurias, the count of Ampurias, together with Roger de Lauria, the count of Pallars, Ramón Folch, and several knights, traveling swiftly by another road, went to the monastery of the town of Rosas. There was a multitude of French there, with a copious store of food and other necessities. They captured the town and monastery with all these stores, but not without the slaughter of many of the French.

With the king of France thus retreating with his downcast army from the county of Ampurias, the men of the king of Aragon divided themselves into a number of contingents and harried them with numerous attacks, one right after the other, now from the rear, now from the left, now from the right, so that the French did not know what part of their army most needed reinforcements. That day, in pain and peril, they reached the place of La Junquera. So many of them had been killed on the road that one could not march except on the bodies of the slain, and the victors were able to pick up jewelry and other spoils by the roadside shrine.

As the enemy were encamped that night at the place of La Junquera, King Pedro and his knights decided that, since the French army was so reduced and was leaving the kingdom, they would attack them in force at their camp. Through that night, Pedro made preparations for the execution of his plans. Thus it was that, when the French took the road at daybreak and were in the pass of Panissars, King Pedro and his men were at their rear. They attacked them so sharply that many of the French fell in this assault, and the others were pursued at sword point. This pursuit lasted until they had descended the pass and were near the castle of Montesquieu. The greatest slaughter of Frenchmen took place on that day.[312]

King Pedro assembled his men and found that he had not lost any of them nor had any been injured, although they were fatigued by the labors they had performed that day. The French were wounded and beaten, and they directed their steps to Perpignan, where the king of France and many of his men ended their last days.[313] According to an acceptable estimate, of the men who had come in aid of the king of France, not a twentieth part had survived. Not that many would have escaped if the nobles, knights, and citizenry of the places of Aragon had aided King Pedro, their lord, when he was placed in such straits. No matter how many times they were called to arms by him before the arrival of the king of France, they refused to respond. They alleged that, inasmuch as the king was not preserving their privileges, liberties, and immunities for them, they would not do for him those things that they were bound and held to do. Following the protestations that the Aragonese made to King Pedro, their lord, they publicly announced that, if he would not preserve their privileges and immunities, they would select another lord. This king, like a stout monarch, refused to accept this, and they refused to assist him.

The nobles, knights, burgesses, and men of the towns of Aragon assembled at the city of Zaragoza to discuss the maintenance of their privileges, liberties, and laws. There they established a union among themselves, agreeing that they would be unanimous and act as one against King Pedro, their lord, and against any other who might oppose their laws, liberties, and privileges. This was the first union that the Aragonese made. At length they were disobedient to their lord, and many evils and disturbances ensued from this.

And behold the result of the pompous enterprise undertaken by the king of France and King Charles, who entitled himself "King of Aragon" before the day when he entered Aragon and took possession of it!

King Pedro, exultant and rejoicing at such an illustrious victory, returned to the spoils that they had captured from the enemy. There was such an exorbitant quantity of arms, jewelry, and other things, that all Catalunya was made rich and full of joy by it.

King Pedro did not covet any of these things, but generously permitted his subjects to take them all.

Despite their confused and disordered state, the French continued to garrison the city of Girona. They had agreed with their king, however, that unless he came to their aid within a certain period, they could surrender the city to Alfonso, first-born son of King Pedro. When they had received no assistance from the king of France by the agreed-upon time, they had to abandon the city. They surrendered it to Alfonso, who had it solidly rebuilt, which it needed since it had been demolished and burnt.

King Pedro sired four sons and two daughters with his wife. They were named as follows: the first, Alfonso, was king after the death of his father; the second, Jaime, was king of Sicily after the death of his father, and king of Aragon later; the third, Federico, was king of Sicily, as we shall recount more fully below; and the fourth, Pedro. Of the daughters, the first was Isabella, who married the king of Portugal; the second was Constanza, who remained with her mother and her brother, Jaime, in the kingdom of Sicily, and married Robert, king of Sicily and Jerusalem.[314]

The victorious king stayed in his lands, excessively fatigued by the multitudinous labors he had sustained in the matters previously discussed. He ordered Charles, prince of Salerno, who was being held prisoner in Sicily with many of his barons, nobles, and knights, to be transferred to

Catalunya, since he could be kept under better guard there than in Sicily. When Charles arrived at the new castle of Barcelona, Pedro ordered that he be closely guarded. After still further consideration of his custody, the king sent Charles under close guard to the castle of Ciurana, situated in the county of Prades and extremely well fortified. He stayed here for a long time under the closest custody.

This matter having been settled, the king turned his attention to the treachery of King Jaime of Mallorca, which we have narrated at greater length above. He ordered an immense fleet to be prepared to sail to Mallorca against his brother Jaime. But the fleet was not yet ready when the king fell gravely ill in Villafranca del Panadés. He arranged that his first-born son, Alfonso, should implement the plan in his place and conquer the kingdom of Mallorca. He fondly asked this of Alfonso in the presence of all his men gathered in council. Alfonso was brought to accept the undertaking entrusted to him by the affectionate entreaties of his father.

The fleet was made ready, and Alfonso sailed to the city of Mallorca with many knights and infantry.[315] He finally established control over it and the entire kingdom of Mallorca. He expelled from the city Pons of Guardia, who had been governor in the kingdom of Mallorca for King Jaime, as well as all other persons who had held power there for him.

With King Alfonso reigning in the kingdom of Mallorca, the virtuous King Pedro, in the fifty-fifth year of his age, following a humble confession and act of contrition for his sins, rendered up his spirit to the Creator in Villafranca del Panadés in the Year of Our Lord 1283.[316] He had ruled seven years, three months, and nineteen days.

Although the land had received from him all the commandments due from a Christian and had been left under a good administration, at his death it was nevertheless in great distress and peril, at war with the Church and the more powerful princes of the world. The king was publicly interred in a sepulcher in the church of the monastery of Santas Creus, of the Cistercian order.

He reigned in a praiseworthy fashion and always triumphed over his enemies. Because of his death, his entire land was in sorrow, tears, and lamentation, which lasted for nine years.

His wife and children, who were in Sicily, indulged in deep and long sobbing and sighs together with all the rest of the island. The queen, together with the barons, nobles, knights, and populace of the kingdom of Sicily then held a general court at Palermo. With unanimous agreement, they there chose Jaime, son of King Pedro and the queen, as their king and lord. His selection was the greatest consolation for the Sicilians, having a king descended from the seed of so very virtuous a king.

Chapter 37
KING ALFONSO [III, 1285–1291] AND HIS DEEDS, AND THE CAPTURE OF MENORCA

The sad death of so excellent a king being known, Alfonso, his first-born son, then ruled. He was surnamed el Magnánimo ["the Generous"] because as long as he lived among the princes of the world, he gave much largess.

He was in the city of Mallorca, having wrested the kingdom from his uncle, Jaime, because he had aided the king of France against his brother, King Pedro. He there announced the sorrowful death of his father to the Mallorcans. Through the city and kingdom of Mallorca, there swelled the bitter lamentations of all the people, and sobs broke forth from all breasts.

Having set the affairs of the kingdom of Mallorca in good order, Alfonso went to Catalunya to accept the royal crown. He then ordered a general court to be held in the city of Zaragoza, and there was crowned and chosen as king according to the custom observed by the other kings of Aragon up to the present time.[317]

The Aragonese obtained from him, more by their force than his grace,[318] his praise and approbation of the union which they had formed in the time of King Pedro, together with his charter sealed with a leaden bulla as a memorial for the future.

The assembly having been held, he departed. He then lent a willing ear to several Aragonese nobles and knights in his service who were opposed to this union. Because of this issue, there was a great conflict throughout his life between the king and the defenders of the union, a coalition he was never able to overcome. On the contrary, the kingdom almost came to ruin because of it.

The Aragonese declared on a certain day that they would obey Charles of Valois, of whom we spoke above in the deeds of King Pedro. The Roman pontiff named him king of Aragon. The Aragonese did not put their decision into effect, however, because Alfonso agreed to whatever they asked of him. In addition to many other things contrary to justice, they asked and obtained from him the privilege that, if he did not protect the privileges he had granted them concerning their union and the ordinances he had made regarding it, they could select another king and expel him from the realm. And they could do the same to his successors if they did not respect these privileges.[319]

After some time had elapsed, King Alfonso became eager to follow in the praiseworthy footsteps of his predecessors, and went to the island of Menorca with a great body of cavalry and infantry, and placed it under his dominion. When the blind Mohammedan perversity had been rooted out of the island, he held up the light of the Orthodox Faith there.[320] This Alfonso struck up a friendship with Alfonso of Castile,[321] who had been disinherited by his uncle Sancho in the following manner. This disinherited Alfonso was the son of Prince Fernando, the first-born brother of Sancho. Fernando had taken a daughter of the king of France as wife, from whom he had sired two sons, Alfonso and Fernando. Their father, Fernando, had died while his own father yet lived. After the death of his father, Alfonso of Castile, Sancho, the second son, ruled. Alfonso the Disinherited ought to have ruled since he was the son of the first-born Prince Fernando. Because of this, he was called "the Disinherited."

This Alfonso was elected king of Castile in the city of Jaca, with King Alfonso of Aragon and Gaston of Bearne present.[322] They all went to Castile to place the chosen one in possession of his realm.[323] Diego of Vizcaya and others of the realm of Castile, and about three hundred cavalry, were with Alfonso of Castile. There were four thousand cavalry with the king of Aragon. They reached a place called Monteagudo de las Vicarias.

King Sancho of Castile assembled his army against them. There were ten thousand cavalry in this force, although there were friends of Alfonso of Castile among them. When all sides stood prepared for battle, the Castilians found a means to avoid fighting. They asked Alfonso of Castile to postpone the day of fighting to the morrow and said that they would then take an oath to him as lord and king. He granted them this. The Castilians fled in the night, however, and King Alfonso of Aragon invaded Castile, laying it waste. While he was doing this, he received letters from the king of England, whom he considered as a father because he had married a daughter of his.[324] In order to meet with him and hold council, Alfonso desisted from his enterprise and withdrew from Castile.[325] A day and place was then fixed on which he and the king of England could each be present as honorably prepared as each was able.

Among the various projects discussed was that King Alfonso should release King Charles, whom he held prisoner, so that Charles could personally arrange a peace between Alfonso and the Church and the other princes who were his enemies.[326] But Alfonso required that Robert and Louis, two of Charles's sons, and seven of the nobler barons of Provence and Naples should first be turned over as hostages.

When this project was put into effect, King Alfonso, on the advice of Charles, sent solemn heralds to arrange peace. It was now his plan not to rest until peace was proclaimed by the Roman pontiff, Nicholas IV [1288–1292], and until all sides were commanded that it be obeyed.[327]

But an unfortunate event befell King Alfonso while he was in Barcelona. Having invited prelates and nobles, knights and other people, he had prepared a festive and solemn feast. It was on a fine morning, which turned into a deplorable one. He arose from bed and, wishing to ride with lance aloft through the city with many knights drawn up to accompany him, he mounted a horse saddled and bedecked with various ornaments. When he began to urge his horse with his boots, he felt a deep stab of pain in his body.[328] Turning pale, he ordered himself to be taken down from his horse and placed in a bed in the palace. As a result of this accident, not many days later he died like a true Catholic, in the twenty-seventh year of his age, the 1291st of the Lord, having humbly donned the habit of Saint Francis.[329] He was buried with honor and sorrow in the church of the Friars Minor in Barcelona. His brother, Jaime, then king of Sicily, was instated as his heir in accordance with the succession ordained by their father, Pedro, in his last testament.

This King Alfonso reigned seven years, eight months, and six days, during which he neither married nor sired children.[330]

Chapter 38

KING JAIME [II, 1291–1327] AND HIS DEEDS, AND THE PEACE HE MADE WITH THE KING OF FRANCE

When King Alfonso was dead, all of Catalunya, together with the other kingdoms, decided that the count of Ampurias should go to Sicily with two armed galleys and an armed galleas to announce the sorrowful death of King Alfonso and to provide transport to King Jaime of Sicily, known as "the Justiciar" because he never allowed anyone besides himself to sit in judgment of disputes.

The count went to Sicily and explained the cause of his coming to King Jaime of Sicily, and to the Queen Mother. They and all Sicily indulged in great moans and lamentations. When calm was restored, and Jaime had appointed his brother Federico as governor in Sicily, the king sailed in the galleys with the count to Barcelona. He was there acclaimed ruler and honored.[331]

He first had masses celebrated throughout Catalunya and all his kingdoms, and distributed many alms to the poor for the souls of his father, Pedro, and brother, Alfonso. He then decreed that a general court should meet in Zaragoza, to which the archbishop of Tarragona and many bishops and prelates; and barons, nobles, and knights; and burgesses and the populace came in copious numbers. Jaime was there elevated and crowned king of Aragon, an act that was celebrated in the fashion of the general court and with solemn festivity. Constitutions and ordinances concerning the good of the common weal were issued in this assembly.[332]

After some days, the king of Castile gave his daughter María to King Jaime as wife, despite the fact that she was in a close degree of consanguinity with him, a fact that Jaime considered gravely. Because of the great advantage of the match and the promises that the king of Castile made to the king of Aragon, and believing that he would get aid and favor from him against his enemies, however, Jaime consented to this matrimony wholeheartedly. The king of Castile promised Jaime that the Supreme Pontiff would grant a dispensation for the marriage, and that he would never abandon him confronting the Church and his other enemies.[333]

But behold what an evil end this promise of assistance from the king of Castile had! When King Jaime of Aragon, King Sancho of Castile, King Charles of Naples, and Jaime of Mallorca, King Jaime's uncle, were at Logroño to discuss the peace being arranged by King Charles between King Jaime of Aragon and the Church and the other kings who were his enemies, the king of Castile was corrupted by the offer of a large amount of money made to him by King Charles. They held a secret meeting or discussion and debated whether by some means the king of Castile could capture King Jaime and deliver him as a prisoner to King Charles so that the sons of Charles and the barons whom Jaime held imprisoned might be released without their having to conclude a peace. Through his own sagacity and the help of God, Jaime learned of these dealings, but kept his knowledge a secret. Taking the queen, his wife and the daughter of the king of Castile, he returned to his own lands.[334]

The queen may have been of an age to allow the consummation of their marriage. Nevertheless, carnal knowledge between the two did not ensue, despite the fact that the king of Castile, through solemn messengers, often requested that it should. But he had not obtained the dispensation that he had promised to secure from the pope on the day set for it, nor afterward. Knowing this, King Jaime was unwilling to consummate the marriage between himself and the daughter of the king of Castile through carnal knowledge, but he held and treated her with the honor due a queen. She was thus kept apart from him until peace was made between him and the Church and King Charles. A marriage was then celebrated between him and King Charles's daughter, Blanche.[335]

King Charles, seeing that he would not be able to make the progress he wanted through this project of his, tried another method.[336] He strove so that a peace would in fact be agreed upon. He arranged a conference in Catalunya, in the plain which surrounds the castle of Montroig, in which he and King Jaime discussed the matter. They agreed between themselves upon this peace, the provisions of which they set down in precise articles. These articles were then closed and sealed with the seals of each king.[337] King Charles took them with him and showed them to the Roman pontiff in full consistory, because the Roman pontiff had to give his consent to them.

When the articles had been read and understood, King Jaime sent his special emissaries to Boniface [VIII, 1295–1303], the Roman pontiff, for the ratification of the peace. The Roman pontiff, together with his cardinals, King Charles, and the emissaries, signed them and drew them up in the required form.[338]

The Roman pontiff immediately commanded Cardinal Guillelmo of Ferreris to go to Catalunya, and to the kingdoms and other lands of King Jaime, to proclaim the peace and to revoke the interdict that had lain over these territories for fourteen years.

When this had been ordered, the cardinal set out, along with King Charles and his daughter Blanche. While they were tarrying at the town of Perpignan to refresh themselves, the cardinal became gravely ill. Within a few days, he had reached the end of his life, and was buried with honor in the monastery of the Friars Minor of that town.

King Jaime had wished to go out to meet the party, but was detained by illness in the town of Girona. Because of the death of the cardinal and the illness of the king, it was necessary to postpone the publication of the peace.

King Charles immediately informed the Supreme Pontiff of the cardinal's death, begging him to send another in his place. The Supreme Pontiff, grieving at the death of the cardinal, appointed and dispatched in his place the archbishops of Embrun and Arles, commanding them to finish the cardinal's mission jointly and to promulgate the peace.

King Charles, with his daughter and the archbishops, and King Jaime, with his barons and knights, arrived at Vilabertrán on the day of the festival of All-Saints [1 November], in the Year of Our Lord 1295. The archbishops published the peace on that day, absolved King Jaime and all who were with him and forgave him and his subjects all injuries and damages inflicted by them upon the Church, the king of France and his subjects, or any other king or person as a result of the conflict. They also suspended and revoked the interdict that had lain over Jaime's lands and places.

King Jaime then took Blanche, daughter of King Charles, as his wife, in fulfillment of an agreement in the articles of peace, designed to strengthen them and assure their better observance.[339] When these things had been done, King Jaime unconditionally freed from their prisons King Charles's sons and the barons whom he had held captive as hostages for King Charles. He renounced all rights and claims that he had or might have had, for whatever reason, in the kingdom of Sicily, as he had agreed in the articles mentioned above.

He ordered the Sicilian emissaries, who had come there for this occasion, henceforth to obey the Church. When the emissaries heard the order given them, they tore their garments in full view of the king and, moved by anger, they broke out in many disrespectful words. They then said to him, "Lord King, may it please your lordship to give us a lord, or to tell us whom you wish us to choose. We have seen, and have heard talked about, many vassals who abandoned their lord. But a lord deserting his vassals, as you have done to us, was unheard of until now!"

Like desperate men, they uttered many other words against King Jaime, urging him not to commit such a breach of faith. Again they said to him, "Lord King, you say that you wish us to choose a lord. You yourself give us a king, because it is you who is abandoning us." The king, with a bitter inner grief, said to them, "Our brother Federico remains in Sicily as governor. Do as you wish." The emissaries then went with their men and colored all their galleys, sails, and even their rigging black, and attired themselves and all their entourage in black clothes. And thus they returned to Sicily and told Federico what had befallen them. The nobles and commoners of Sicily immediately assembled and unanimously chose Federico as their king. He, however, stayed away from these discussions about choosing a king, since he was ruling for his brother, Jaime.[340]

Some time after this deliberation, Pope Boniface and King Charles conferred on how to arrange a peace between the Church and Federico. After various proposals, the Roman pontiff promised Federico that within a certain time he would give him the daughter of the emperor of Constantinople, nephew of King Charles, as his wife. Afterward, at the expense of the Church, he would acquire the empire of Constantinople, since it belonged to his future wife by hereditary right. The condition was added, however, that Federico would not oppose the Church for the kingdom of Sicily, nor would he go through with his coronation.

Beset by accidents, the Supreme Pontiff was not able to make good the various promises he had made within the time he had specified. Federico, because of the urgent pleas of the Sicilians, accepted the crown of the kingdom of Sicily and was their king and lord.[341]

Some days later, King Jaime and Queen Blanche went to inland Catalunya and, by order of the pope, sent to the king of Castile, with only mediocre honors and not the queenly splendor due the daughter of a king, the daughter who had been espoused to King Jaime and of whom we spoke above.

When these things had been done and an armed fleet prepared, King Jaime and a band of many noble men went to Rome to visit the threshold of the Apostles, Saints Peter and Paul, and to appear before the Roman pontiff.[342] King Charles, with all the cardinals and many Roman citizens, was overjoyed at his coming and received him with honors and festivities. When he had done reverence to the Supreme Pontiff and had visited the shrines, on a certain day scheduled for this, the Supreme Pontiff, the kings, and cardinals held a secret conference.

It was agreed between the pope and cardinals that King Jaime should be the arm and defense of the Roman Church, its banner-bearer and admiral, and that he should subjugate Sicily to the Church.[343] The Supreme Pontiff then granted King Jaime the conquest and acquisition of Sardinia and Corsica, and the tithes of his realms and lands for four years.[344] And he granted him other things. On his part, King Jaime gave his sister, called Violant, as wife to Robert, son of King Charles.

When all was thus completed, King Jaime returned to his own land with great honor. There, with the counsel of his nobles, knights, and all his citizens, he assembled a great band of cavalry and infantry, attacked the kingdom of Murcia with great force, and acquired it for his dominion.

In these times, King Jaime's brother, Prince Pedro, a particularly strong man, rose up against King Fernando of Castile [IV, 1295–1312] and supported Alfonso the Disinherited, of whom we spoke above in the deeds of the previous Alfonso, king of Aragon.[345] Supporting him were Jimeno d'Urrea, Pedro Cornel, Pedro Fernández of Azagra, lord of Albarracín, and other nobles of Aragon. Prince Juan, uncle of the king of Castile, and the king of Portugal also invaded Castile, laying it waste in various ways. While they were passing through the kingdom of Leon, sickness broke out among them, from which many died, including Prince Pedro of Aragon, who died during the siege of Oter de Humos.

After his death, the Aragonese immediately returned to Aragon with Fernando's children, carrying the corpse of Prince Pedro to Zaragoza, where it was placed in a tomb in the chapter house of the Friars Minor.

The king of Portugal retired to his kingdom for his part, and, of those mentioned above, it was Jimeno of Urrea who stoutly visited so many evils on Castile that, from these times on, he inspired a particular turn of speech in Castile. When someone wants to say a bad word to someone else, he says to him, "May the Urreas pass through your house to your ruin!" What he did there is measured by these words.

When the kingdom of Murcia had been taken from the king of Castile by King Jaime and added to his own dominions, and the necessary officials installed in it, King Jaime returned to Catalunya with joy and honor.[346]

The Roman pontiff sent messengers calling upon him, on the strength of the agreement struck between them a short time before, to assemble a body of as many cavalry and infantry as he could and, at the Church's expense, to go to Sicily to subjugate it to the Church. Since the king could not dispute the terms of the treaty, once having received a stipend, he boarded the fleet prepared for this at the place of Palamos with a great force of his barons, knights, and infantry and went directly to Rome. He was honorably received by the Roman pontiff, cardinals, and other citizens there.

He tarried there for some days, and it was arranged in what fashion the king should conduct this affair. He left there with his wife Blanche, King Charles, and one legate appointed by the pope to collect his stipend. He arrived in Naples, where the queen gave birth to a son, who was named Alfonso. While he was there, he secretly notified his brother Federico what he ought to do: to wit, that he should never appear in Jaime's presence, but should guard and fortify his land well. He should fear nothing, for Jaime had not agreed to occupy Sicily in this undertaking, but to satisfy the promises he had made.

Despite the fact that the Sicilians knew this, they suggested to Federico that he should defend his realm with a mighty battle, and that he do battle against his brother by sea. Federico did not hesitate, but, with a countless multitude of his men, boarded the galleys which he had prepared for this purpose. They were sixty in number, and there were many Aragonese and Catalans among his followers.

There were scarcely any nobles or knights with King Jaime who did not have brothers or sons with King Federico well prepared for battle. The Aragonese and Catalans who were with King Jaime therefore hesitated, and advised him not to fight. Wishing to fulfill the promises he had made, the king told them that they should have no fear on this account, because the greater and better men were with him, and he did not believe that his subjects would wage war on him. It is said that, at these words, a number of his followers threw themselves into the sea in the presence of the king of Aragon, their natural lord.[347]

Seeing that his brother Federico wholeheartedly wished to do battle with him, the king sent a messenger to him on an armed ship. The messenger reiterated that Federico should refuse to depend upon the doubtful outcome of battle, since his brother Jaime would of a certainty conduct himself in such a way that the kingdom of Sicily would not be endangered by his coming. But when he had heard all these worthy admonitions, King Federico was still unwilling to renounce his tenacious and obstinate plans. King Jaime first made a restriction that no one except his subjects was allowed to board the galleys, which were fifty in number, because he wished to do battle against his brother with a force limited in this fashion to his own vassals.

When these things were done and his wife had been sent to Naples, the king boarded the galleys with his subjects, it always being in his heart to avoid a confrontation with his brother, if it were possible for him to do so. But his brother, at the constant urging of the Sicilians, hastened to his hostile confrontation with King Jaime. The galleys of both kings mingled in combat, the battle fought so bitterly that the sea was dyed with the blood of those struck. Finally, with the aid of the right hand of God, the Sicilian galleys were defeated, and King Federico's galley fled. The few others that were left were captured, and even Federico's ship was soon taken, but the victorious king ordered his brother to withdraw.

King Jaime was pierced through the foot with an arrow in this battle. He had wanted to stand with his foot on the roof of the galley. During the battle, he did not move his foot from the place where it had been nailed, nor did he disclose to anyone that he was wounded, which was a marvel to all.

It is said that some of his followers suggested to the king that he should charge with treason and hold as traitors any of his subjects who were with King Federico in battle against him. He answered them by declaring publicly that there were many other traitors back in Aragon and Catalunya. It is true that there were many of his lineage and service who had remained in Aragon. He exiled them from his realms and confiscated their property, but then transferred these properties to their relatives.

Rendering thanks to God, he came to Sicily with his entire fleet. When he was there, the legate and the French who had remained in Naples came to Sicily with great rejoicing. While they deliberated what was to be done next in pursuit of their enterprise, someone told the king, in the presence of the legate, that a nearby castle would surrender to him if he would go out to it. This made the king sad at heart, but he hid his sadness so that it might appear to the legate that he truly had it in his heart to subjugate the kingdom of Sicily.

Leaving that place, he came to the castle, which was surrendered to him by a castellan of his to whom it had been entrusted. The king immediately had him hanged for a certain crime he had once committed against him. When this had been done, some members of the legate's entourage came to the king, saying that the castellan of another castle would surrender it to him if he saw him present there. Approaching the castle, the king held his right arm before him and, opening his hand, said, "You scoundrel, surrender this castle to me or I'll have you hanged!" The castellan, however, interpreting the king's desires, knew that the king did not wish him to surrender the castle to him, and said, "Get out of range or I will drive you off; you have been a traitorous lord to us!" Saying this, the castellan, who had had many ballistae strung, began to load them with arrows.

Meanwhile, the time for payment of the stipend had arrived, but the legate did not have the necessary money, no matter how much was daily sent to him. The king and his army therefore withdrew and sailed to Barcelona. First, however, he ordered a certain knight of his, Bertrán of Canellis by name and a resident of Panadés, to go to King Charles with two galleys and to convey the queen, his wife Blanche, to Catalunya. When the knight explained the cause of his coming to King Charles, the king said to him, "The king of Aragon certainly did not conduct himself faithfully in this affair, because he could have subjugated the kingdom of Sicily had he wished." The knight answered him, "If, God save me, anyone asserts this, he is lying falsely through his beard!" And he thereupon declared himself ready to defeat any asserting the contrary one after the other in combat, proclaiming that the king of Aragon had acted in this matter legally and just as he ought to have done. No one challenged him. King Charles then ordered the queen for whom he had come to be turned over to him.

After this knight's departure, King Charles called the knights and others who were present at the knight's declaration together and said to them, "O knights, did it not strike any of you as disgraceful and shameful that this Catalan knight should have called me a liar in your presence and that none of you would challenge him? Does this happen with the knights of Aragon? Certainly not!" Then all of them arose to accept the challenge. He told them, "Is it the time now, when the knight has departed? God help me, this is a great dishonor for me, and for you."

After some time, Dinis, king of Portugal, wished for peace and harmony between the kings of Castile and Aragon, and these three kings gathered at Tarazona to negotiate. Peace and union was established among them, and their hostility was turned against the king of Granada. King Jaime restored the city of Murcia to the king of Castile, but retained possession of Orihuela, Guardamar, Alicante, Elche and Crevillente, La Muela, the valleys of Elda and Novella, and other castles situated in Painted Rocks.[348] The king of Castile gave his daughter as wife to Prince Jaime, first-born son of King Jaime, despite the fact that both of them were of quite tender ages. After these deliberations, each of them began to implement that which had been agreed upon between them.[349]

Having prepared a great fleet to besiege Almería powerfully by land and sea, King Jaime took his wife, Blanche, with him. The King of Castile made similar preparations for taking the city of Alcira de Alfadra [Algeciras].[350] The city of Almería was besieged by the king of Aragon, and there were many sharp assaults. A large number of Saracens, both cavalry and infantry, came over from Africa. Loosing loud ululations, they attacked the forces of the king of Aragon, attempting to break the siege if they could. Through his virtue and the great and outstanding strength of his men, the king attacked them bravely, and courageously put them to flight. The pursuit and slaughter of the Saracens lasted without stop all day. According to a common estimate, six thousand Saracens, cavalry and infantry, perished by the sword that day, it being the feast of Saint Bartholomew the Apostle [24 August] in the Year of Our Lord 1309. The king happily renewed the siege, praising God that his men were well and that none were disabled.

The city of Almería then found itself hard-pressed. Another swarm of Saracens then came upon the king and his men. With God bringing fortune, he defeated them with even greater success and distinction than before, and more were slain than the first time. Those who escaped by dint of running away retreated sadly and mournfully.

Clearly seeing his ruin and that of his people, the king of Granada intervened with an immense sum of money and, through the mediation of certain barons of Castile, negotiated with the king of Castile to abandon his siege and return home. When an agreement had been reached, the king of Castile announced the fact to the king of Aragon through his messengers.[351] Seeing that, without assistance from the king of Castile, he could not continue the siege without serious risk, King Jaime negotiated a peace with the king of Granada.

One day while the peace was being discussed, a certain Saracen, who was a mediator in the talks, came to King Jaime with thirty light cavalry. He told the king that he wished to talk to him, and that the king's entourage should withdraw so that he might discuss the peace secretly. The king immediately ordered his men to retire and stayed alone with the Saracens, with whom he had a long conversation. This disturbed his men deeply, and they thought him foolish because of the many dangers that might have befallen him. Having gathered his men, he immediately boarded his ships and returned to Catalunya, painfully perplexed because of the way the king of Castile had treated the promises he had made to him. A transgression of this sort was not a new thing with the Castilians, for treating oaths in this fashion is almost hereditary with them. This custom was implanted in them and passed into their nature, which is why they cannot abstain from such behavior.

When King Jaime left Almería, a great sickness was breaking out in his host and it was helpful for his army to retire. Juan Jiménez of Urrea, lord of Monteagudo, died on the return and was placed in a tomb in the church of the Dominicans in Calatayud. Then the sun was eclipsed on the feast of the Purification of the Blessed Mary [2 February], in the Year of Our Lord 1310.

In this year, Blanche, the king's wife, died. He sired five sons and five daughters by her. Their names were as follows. The first was Jaime, who lived for a time, renounced his kingdom, and refused to consummate the marriage contracted between him and Eleanora, daughter of the king of Castile. The second was Alfonso, who was the count of Urgell and had as wife the daughter of the noble Gombau of Etença, nephew of Ermengol, count of Urgell, and who was king of Aragon after a short while. The third was Juan, who was archbishop of Toledo, and later patriarch of Alexandria and archbishop of Tarragona. The fourth was Pedro, who was count of Ribagorza and Ampurias. When he was fifty-four years of age, he gathered together all his children and took the habit of Saint Francis in the church of the monastery of the Friars Minor at Barcelona, on Monday, the twelfth day of September, in the Year of Our Lord 1353. The fifth was Ramón Berenguer in the county of Prades. We will discuss them more copiously in the life of each below.

The first of the daughters was called María, and she was the wife of Pedro, prince of Castile; the second, Constanza, who was the wife of Juan, son of Prince Manuel of Castile; the third, Isabel, who was the wife of the duke of Austria; the fourth, Blanche, was prioress of the convent of Sigena; the fifth, Violant, was the wife of the son of the prince of Morea and Tarentum. After his death, she married Lope of Luna, lord of Segorbe, who, in the time of King Pedro, was made count of Luna by the king, who gave him Luna at that time.

After the lapse of some time, and after the death of Queen Blanche, King Jaime took as wife María, sister of the king of Cyprus, by whom he sired no offspring because he was of too advanced an age. She lived with King Jaime a short time.[352]

While King Jaime was still alive, his uncle, King Jaume of Mallorca, died. He was a man of great probity and able administration. He doubled his patrimony, which he governed with great justice and rectitude. Surviving him were four sons and two daughters. The first son was called Jaume, who renounced his kingdom while his father was still alive and, having assumed the religious habit, entered the order of Saint Francis. The second was Sanç, who was king; the third, Ferran; and the fourth Fileu, who was of a devout and holy life and left this world a Friar Minor. The first daughter was called Isabel, and she was the wife of Juan Manuel after the death of Jaime, king of Aragon. The other was Sança, who was wife of King Robert. When Jaume, king of Mallorca, died, his second son ruled in his kingdom and lands, because the eldest had renounced his succession to enter religious orders, as has been said.

Jaime, king of Aragon, called for the presence of Sanç, king of Mallorca, in the general court that he celebrated in the city of Girona. Wishing to comply with the will of the king, as he was held by law to do, Sanç came honorably to the city where all the prelates, nobles, knights, and syndics of all the cities and towns of Catalunya were gathered. In their presence, King Sanç of Mallorca was confessed, and recognized that he held the kingdom of Mallorca with its isles, the counties of Rosselló and Cerdanya, and also the barony of Montpellier, in fief from King Jaime of Aragon. He did homage to him for this and gave the oath of fidelity for himself and his men, and public documents were drawn up attesting this.

It was then decided that Alfonso, son of King Jaime, count of Urgell, and his general procurator should go to put an end to the kingdom of Sardinia and Corsica. Promises of aid in the execution of this affair were not wanting from King Sanç of Mallorca. He offered twenty armed galleys to use, and had them prepared, at his own expense, to be sent in aid of Alfonso.

When this court had been celebrated, King Jaime went to Tarragona. Here he took as wife Elisenda of Montcada, on the feast of the Nativity of Our Lord [25 December], in the Year of Our Lord 1322. On the same day, in Barcelona, his son Alfonso publicly unfurled the fleet's banner for the expedition to Sardinia.

Jaime later came to Barcelona and, at the suggestion of the noble Ugo, judge of Arborea and viscount of Basso, sent three ships to Oristan in the island of Sardinia. The ships carried the nobles Dalmacio, viscount of Rocabertí, Bertrán of Castelleto, and Huc of Santa Pau with one hundred and eighty cavalry in the month of May, in the Year of Our Lord 1323. This was done because the commune of Pisa had sent a body of cavalry and infantry to Sardinia in its defense.

In this same month, Alfonso embarked from the city of Barcelona with twenty armed galleys and a fleet of cargo ships and other naval vessels to go to Portfangós, where the day was scheduled on which the troops were to come and board ship. King Jaime was there in person with all his children, and many prelates and nobles of Catalunya, Aragon, and the kingdom of Valencia. Also Huc of Totzo, admiral of Sanç, king of Mallorca, came with twenty galleys manned by Sanç's troops. And there were many other squadrons for carrying knights, horses, infantry, and siege equipment.

Alfonso left port with the first day of June of this year drawing near, taking his wife, Teresa, with him, and with sixty galleys, twenty-four ships, and many other naval vessels numbering about three hundred or more.[353] On the fifth day of the month of June, he was in the port of Mahon, on the island of Menorca, where the weather had carried him. When he learned that the Pisans had sent cavalry and infantry to the island of Sardinia, he decided to board his galley and to be in Sardinia quickly with the swift galleys.[354] Thus it was done.

Leaving this port with all his galleys and others of the fleet on the ninth day of June, on the thirteenth of the same month he was with the galleys at the cape of San Marco, near Oristan, on the island of Sardinia. He was there informed by the judge of Arborea that the noble viscount of Rocabertí, and the others who had come over earlier in the three ships, were at a place called Quarto Sant'Elena, a league distant from the castle of Cagliari, with troops which the judge had sent them in order to prevent food from being sent into the castle.

Alfonso decided to transfer himself to the port of Palma de Sols. He sent an armed lighter back to tell the fleet that they should set the same course. When the whole fleet had assembled, Alfonso first besieged Iglesia de Cixerri, which he took, although not without great labor.[355]

On Ash Wednesday in the Year of Our Lord 1323, he had a battle with his enemies, who numbered more than thirteen hundred knights and two thousand crossbowmen, under the command of Manfredo, count of Noratico. Although Alfonso had only four hundred and ninety-three knights and a thousand infantry, almost all of whom were weak, he gained a victory over his opponents. Between knights and infantry, more than twelve hundred were killed, but of Alfonso's men, only six knights and six foot soldiers. With the palm of praise, he carried off spoils from their camp and raised praises to God for having given him such a miraculous triumph.[356]

He then went to besiege the castle of Cagliari. While he was holding it under close siege, one day after dinner, when the unsuspecting besiegers had fallen asleep, all of those in the castle made a sally against the besiegers and quickly broke into their ranks. The work of God was manifest and miraculous in this affair, since forty or so knights and some infantrymen of the besieging force defeated the attackers, who retreated in great dishonor and confusion. More than three hundred of their knights were dead, not counting the infantry. Of Alfonso's, none fell dead save two: Bernat Centelles and Guillem, lord of Monteagudo, whose fighting ardor had rendered him heedless and carried him along with the enemy as they reentered the castle.

On the following day, those in the castle proposed a truce so that they might bury their dead. This was granted to them. They buried those they could, and they used two wells for the rest, piling dirt over them so that the army of the besiegers would not be offended.[357]

Perhaps because of these things, Manfredo asked to meet with Alfonso, since he was a kinsman. Alfonso replied that he could not see him except in battle. Manfredo was later stricken with a sickness of the spirit and expired. To continue, at the end of the month of June, twenty armed galleys came in support of Alfonso, having been sent to him by King Jaime. With their arrival, the enemy in the fortress were overwhelmed by fear, and they began to negotiate. It was agreed between them and Alfonso that the commune of Pisa would give him all of the fortresses it held on the island of

Sardinia; it would hold the fortress of Cagliari in fief from the king of Aragon, and the leaders of Pisa would offer homage for it.[358]

And it was so arranged that, on the twelfth day of July, in the Year of Our Lord 1324, the banner of Prince Alfonso, escorted by a noble band of warriors, was taken into the castle of Cagliari and placed above a gate in the tower of Orifany, while another banner was placed on the bell tower of the cathedral church.

Bernat of Boxadors, knight, and Guillem Olomar, burgess of Barcelona, went to Pisa to accept the homage of the leaders of the Pisan commune. Prince Alfonso ordained that the noble Filippo of Celucra, who came from Sicily, should remain as governor in Sardinia, with two hundred knights and five hundred infantry.

These things having been accomplished, on the eighteenth day of July of the same year, Prince Alfonso retired with all his fleet from the place of Bonayre and went to San Martín, where he stayed for two days. Departing from there, he reached Barcelona on the second day of August, and was received by his father King Jaime and others, with immense joy and honor.

After some time had passed, King Alfonso's wife, Teresa, died.[359] Two sons and a daughter survived her. The first was called Pedro, who took the oath as heir to the kingdom in the city of Zaragoza before Teresa died,[360] just after Alfonso had returned from Sardinia, to be precise. The other was Jaime, who was count of Urgell and viscount of Ager. The daughter was called Constanza, and she was the wife of King Jaume of Mallorca, who, because of the demands of justice, was expelled from his kingdom and lands by Pedro, king of Aragon, his cradle-mate, and brother of Jaume's wife.

Let us return to King Jaime, father of Alfonso. While Jaime still lived, King Sanç of Mallorca left this world. He was a straightforward man and never wished to be an enemy to the House of Aragon, as his mandates demonstrate. He named as his heir Jaume, son of his brother Ferran, who had died in Greece. Because he had been named as heir, with the consent and knowledge of two good men from Mallorca, two from Perpignan, two from Puigcerdá, and all his counselors, King Jaume was given a guardian until he might be able to govern his lands himself.

These representatives selected his uncle, Feliu, as Jaume's guardian. Feliu was unwilling to accept the office of guardian until he was finally compelled to do so by the pope. While he exercised this office and some people refused to obey him, there was great discord among the men of Jaume's realm and lands. But finally, in order to quiet the conflict, Feliu arranged that his nephew, Jaume, should take a daughter of Alfonso as wife. When this was done, the discord was quelled, and Jaume was elevated as king of Mallorca. But he ruled the land more like a tyrant than a king. Because of what he did against his cradle-mate, King Pedro of Aragon, as we shall relate below, he was justly expelled from his kingdom and his lands.

King Jaime of Aragon was very wise and, by his great astuteness, he destroyed the union that the Aragonese had begun in the time of King Pedro, his father, and that had persisted among the Aragonese in the time of Alfonso, Jaime's brother, and even at the beginning of the reign of Jaime himself. For this reason, there was peace and harmony between him and his subjects throughout his lifetime.

King Jaime of Aragon rendered up his spirit to the Creator, in the sixty-fifth year of his life, in the city of Barcelona, on the vigil of All Saints [31 October].[361] He reigned for thirty-seven years, four months, and fourteen days. He was buried with honor in the monastery of Santas Creus in the Year of Our Lord 1327.

He ruled his lands for a long time with justice and mercy, and established his son Alfonso as his heir in the kingdoms of Aragon, Valencia, and Sardinia, and in the county of Barcelona, and he gave him dominion over his brothers, Pedro in the counties of Ribagorza and Ampurias, to which he held title by purchase, and Ramón Berenguer in the county of Prades.

Chapter 39
KING ALFONSO [IV, 1327–1336] AND ALL HIS DEEDS

When King Jaime was dead, his successor in his kingdoms and lands was Alfonso, surnamed "the Benign," because he was more courteous in words and familiar with his subjects than other princes of the world, and because he was like a comrade to them.

When his father had been interred, Alfonso called a court to meet at Zaragoza. Here he was crowned and anointed king with far more honor than any king previously.[362]

He took Eleanora, daughter of King Fernando of Castile, as wife. She had been betrothed to his brother, Prince Jaime, but the marriage had not come into effect because he renounced the succession to enter holy orders.[363] After taking this last wife, Alfonso did nothing worthy of remark, because he was continuously ill.

He sired two sons by this newest wife, one called Fernando, who was marquis of Tortosa, and the other Juan.

While King Alfonso was living, his uncle, King Federico of Sicily, died. He sired three sons from his wife. The first of them was named Pietro and succeeded to the kingdom of Sicily;[364] another was Giovanni and he was duke of Athens; the other was Guillelmo, who died without having received any dignity.

The union that was in revolt in the times of King Alfonso's predecessors was not revived in his time. This was due to the wisdom of his father, Jaime. Utilizing effective means, he laid it to rest; and, because of his great kindness, he restricted the liberties and privileges of the Aragonese as little as possible. In addition, almost all of those who had instigated the union had died.

Alfonso named his son Pedro heir and successor in the kingdoms of Aragon and Valencia, and in the county of Barcelona. He placed his son Jaime, whom he had sired from his first wife, Teresa, in the county of Urgell and the viscounty of Ager. Of the two remaining sons, whom he had sired by his second wife, Eleanora, the elder, called Fernando, inherited the marquisate of Tortosa and the city of Albarracín. The other, called Juan, inherited some lands, but without any title.

In the thirty-seventh year of his life, he rendered up his soul like a true Catholic to his Creator, in the city of Barcelona, on Wednesday, at a half hour to three, it being the vigil of the conversion of Saint Paul [24 January], the eighth of the calends of February, in the Year of Our Lord 1335.

He reigned for eight years, two months, and twenty-four days. And he was buried in the monastery of the Friars Minor in Barcelona.

He was later translated to the monastery of the Friars Minor in the city of Lérida, on the seventeenth day of April, the year of the Nativity of the Lord, 1369, by his son King Pedro.

Thanks be to God.

This book being finished, praise be to the glory of Christ, amen.

Appendix

I: VISIGOTHIC KINGS OF SPAIN

Athaulf	410–415	Liuva II	601–603
Sigeric	415	Witteric	603–610
Wallia	415–419	Gundemar	610–612
Theodoric I	419–451	Sisebut	612–621
Thorismund	451–453	Recared II	621
Theodoric II	453–466	Suinthila	621–631
Euric	466–484	Sisenand	631–636
Alaric II	484–507	Chintila	636–639
Gesalic	507–531	Tulga	639–642
Theodoric II	511–531	Chindasvinth	642–653
Amalric	511–531	Suniefred	?
Theudis	531–548	Recceswinth	642–653
Theudisclus	548–549	Wamba	649–672
Agila I	549–554	Ervig	680–687
Athanagild	551–568	Egica	687–702
Liuva I	568–573	Witiza	698–710
Leovigild	569–586	Roderic	710–711
Recared I	586–601		

II: KINGS OF NAVARRE TO 1035

Iñigo Arista	c. 816–851	García Sánchez I	925–970
García Iñíguez	851–c. 880	Sancho Garcés II	970–994
[García Jiménez]		García Sánchez II	994–1000
Fortún Garcés I	c. 880–905	Sancho Garcés III	1000–1035
Sancho Garcés I	905–925		

III: COUNTS OF ARAGON

[Counts of Aragon]		[Navarrese Hegemony]	
Aznar Galíndez I	809–839	García Sánchez I	925–970
Galindo Aznárez I	c. 830–867	Sancho Garcés II	970–994
Aznar Galíndez II	867–893	García Sánchez II	994–1000
Galindo Aznárez II	893–922	Sancho Garcés III	1000–1035
Andregoto Galíndez	922–925		

IV: KINGS OF ARAGON

Ramiro I	1035–1064	Jaime II	1291–1327
Sancho I	1064–1094	Alfonso IV	1327–1336
Pedro I	1094–1104	Pedro IV	1336–1387
Alfonso I	1104–1134	Juan I	1387–1395
Ramiro II	1134–1137	Martin I	1395–1410
Petronilla	1137–1162	Interregnum	1410–1412
Alfonso II	1162–1196	Fernando I	1412–1416
Pedro II	1196–1213	Alfonso V	1416–1458
Jaime I	1213–1276	Juan II	1458–1479
Pedro III	1276–1285	Fernando II	1479–1516
Alfonso III	1285–1291		

V: COUNTS OF BARCELONA

[French Dependents]

Bera	801–820	Borrell II	947–992
Bernat	820–844	Ramón Borrell	992–1017
Aleran	844–852	Berenguer Ramón I	1017–1035
Salomó	864–873	Ramón Berenguer I	1035–1076
[Independent Counts]		Ramón Berenguer II	1076–1082
Guifred I	870–897	Berenguer Ramón II	1076–1096
Guifred Borrell	897–911	Ramón Berenguer III	1096–1131
Sunyer	911–947	Ramón Berenguer IV	1131–1162

Notes

1. Chapters 1 through 3 depend heavily upon Rodrigo Jiménez de Rada (1180?–1247), *De rebus Hispaniae*, books 1 through 3. Although the compilers do not mention this work specifically, in many places the *Chronicle* is simply an abridgment or rewording of Jiménez. A good edition is available in Rodericus Ximenius de Rada, *Opera* (Textos Medievales no. 22, facsimile reprint of Madrid edition of 1793, Valencia: Anubar, 1968) [cited hereafter as *De rebus Hispaniae*].

2. Referring to Saint Isidore of Seville (560–636), *Historia de regibus Gothorum, Wandalorum et Suevorum*, in *España Sagrada* 6: 481–514, of which a full translation is available in *History of the Kings of the Goths, Vandals and Sueves*, trans. G. Donini and G. B. Ford (2d ed., Leyden: Brill, 1970); and Saint Jerome (ca. 340–420), in his Latin translation of the *Chronikon* of Eusebius.

3. Galatia in Asia Minor.

4. Cicia, a city of Thrace in Greece.

5. Ausonia, an ancient name for southern Italy, later extended to the entire peninsula.

6. Although the conquest of Spain by Hercules is only legendary, early Greek influence through trading towns such as Ampurias on the Gulf of Rosas was an important factor in the development of pre-Roman Iberian culture.

7. A misreading of Scandia.

8. The Alexandrian geographer Claudius Ptolemaeus (fl. 127–141), whom the compilers believe to be two different persons.

9. An excellent survey of this period is available in E. A. Thompson, *The Goths in Spain* (Oxford: Oxford University Press, 1969).

10. The Visigoths in fact conquered Spain from the Alans, Vandals, and Sueves in a lengthy process beginning in 415.

11. The majority of the preceding names are those of the legendary monarchs of the Visigothic people; some are pure inventions.

12. Referring to the period 379 to 396, during which the Visigoths remained relatively pacified by the emperor Theodosius (379–395).

13. The arrangement was made in fact with Alaric's brother Athaulf in 412.

14. The reigns of the Visigothic kings are contained in Appendix I.

15. Actually Liuva I (568–573).

16. The lands involved were territories seized in the reign of the emperor Justinian (527–565) and which had remained under Byzantine control for some time.

17. The Muslim invasion of Spain actually occurred in 711.

18. The territory between Catalunya and the Rhone River in France was

retained by the Visigoths after their defeat at the hands of Clovis at the battle of Vouillé in 507 and the subsequent loss of their other French possessions. The Crown of Aragon would later claim suzerainty of this territory.

19. Referring indirectly to *De rebus Hispaniae*. See note 1.

20. In this and succeeding chapters, the compilers utilize materials from the archives of the monastery of San Juan de la Peña, located about fifteen kilometers southwest of Jaca, and for which the chronicle as a whole has been traditionally named. Chapters 4 through 9 and 11 parallel closely and are almost certainly based upon a short chronicle, written before the thirteenth century and preserved at San Juan de la Peña under the title *La donación de Abetito*. This document has been published by Antonio Durán Gudiol in *Los condados de Aragón y Sobrarbe* (Colección básica aragonesa, no. 51, Zaragoza: Guara Editorial, 1988), pp. 315–319, as *Crónica I de San Juan de la Peña*. Other documentary material from the monastery has been collected in the *Cartulario de San Juan de la Peña*, ed. Antonio Ubieto Arteta (Textos Medievales nos. 6 and 9, Valencia: Anubar, 1962–1963) [hereafter *CSJP*].

21. There is some confusion in the account at this point. San Juan de Pano was in fact located in Sobrarbe.

22. Probably Abd ar-Rahman ibn abd-Allah al-Gafiqi, emir of Córdoba (720–721 and 730–732).

23. Abd al-Malik ibn Khatan was emir of Córdoba in 732 and 739 to 740.

24. The lives of Saints Voto and Felix may be found in the *Acta Sanctorum* (May 7): 63–65.

25. Count Aznar Galíndez II (867–893).

26. García Jiménez was a local chieftain, active probably in the neighborhood of Aibar and Sangüesa, entitled *rex* in some early Aragonese documents. The extent and basis of his authority is unknown, but he would appear to have been contemporary with, rather than prior to, King García Iñíguez (851–c. 880). The dynasty founded by Iñigo Arista ended in 905, and García Jiménez's son, Sancho Garcés (see Chapter 12), took power in obscure circumstances and established a new ruling dynasty.

27. Built near the royal seat of Jaca, Atarés was long a residence in the king's gift and was awarded to that noble most in the royal confidence. The castle no longer exists, but was probably on the site of the present village of Atarés.

28. This donation is recorded in *CSJP* no. 9, dated (9th century?).

29. The date is in error. Given the people cited, the battle in question can only have been the Christian defeat by Abd ar-Rahman III at Val de Junquera in 920.

30. There is no record of any such expedition to Toulouse. It has been suggested that a recollection of a Muslim raid on Tolosa in Navarre may have provided the basis for this statement, but this is only conjecture.

31. The monks of San Juan de la Peña tended to ascribe to their monastery a greater antiquity than it merited. The original foundation, that of Saints Julián and Basilissa, dated probably from about 920 and was the work of Count Galindo Aznárez II. See Antonio Durán Gudiol, *Arte aragonés de los siglos X y XI* (Sabiñánigo: Caja de Ahorros y Monte de Piedad de Zaragoza, Aragón y Rioja, 1973), pp. 18 and 205–208.

32. The compilers were confused on this point, and were probably led astray by

documents such as *CSJP* no. 14, dated 928, which cites King Jimeno Garcés and his *creato* García, and assumed that García was Jimeno's son. If this had been true, the child's full name would have been García Jiménez. Finding no evidence of such a ruler, the chroniclers concluded that the dynasty had become extinct and brought in Iñigo Arista at this point. This introduced serious complications in their chronology, since Iñigo had established his dynasty much earlier, in about 816. Jimeno Garcés (925–931) was in fact the brother of King Sancho Garcés I (905–925). The boy was García Sánchez, son of Sancho Garcés and nephew of Jimeno Garcés, and the actual meaning of *creato* was "ward." The boy succeeded to the throne as García Sánchez I (925–970). This appears to have been the first time in Spanish history that the succession of a minor heir had been secured.

33. The *arista* is the beard of an ear of wheat.

34. This incident is chronologically out of place. Count Fortún Jiménez (934–958) was a contemporary of King García Sánchez I (925–970). It is probable that the donations described here as being confirmed by King García Iñíguez (851–880) were made during the reign of García Sánchez I, close to the date of 959 ascribed to them in the archives of San Juan de la Peña.

35. Thus explaining in part the success against the Muslims attributed to him above.

36. This was an extraordinary privilege, since early Aragon was primarily a pastoral land and the free passage of herds and flocks was a characteristic of the prevailing practices of husbandry. An identical concession had been made by King Fortún Garcés to the nearby monastery of San Julián de Labasal in 893, however. See *CSJP* no. 7, dated 893. This incident of the chronicle was based upon a document that gives every sign of having been a forgery, dating from perhaps the twelfth or thirteenth centuries.

37. The accession of Sancho Garcés I Abarca began a new dynasty in Navarre, that of the Jiménez. The romantic account provided by the *Chronicle* is an expansion of the narrative of *De rebus Hispaniae* 5: 22, and it is clear that the tale owes much to minstrel tales, or *cantares de gesta*.

38. The *abarcas* are the traditional peasant footwear of the western Pyrenees. Covering only part of the foot, they are tied with strings to the calf of the leg.

39. The Montes de Oca were a traditional boundary between Navarre and Castile. See the *Poema de Fernán González* 6: 37–38: "Estonçe era Castyella un pequenno rrincon, / era de castellanos Montes d'Oca mojon."

40. King Alfonso IV of Leon (925–931), King Ramiro II of Leon (931–950), and King Ordoño II of Leon (950–956).

41. In fact, King Sancho Abarca began his reign in 905 and died twenty years later, on 11 October 925.

42. The Navarrese and Aragonese made a clear distinction between royal property and royal authority. García was heir to the property of Sancho Abarca, and succeeded him in royal authority.

43. His soubriquet was actually *el Temblón*, or "the Trembler."

44. The compilers omit mention of Kings Sancho Garcés II (970–994) and García Sánchez II (994–1000).

45. There was no such county of "Portell." Encountering the name of Comes

Diego Porcelli (*De rebus Hispaniae* 5: 25), which translates as "Count Diego, son of Piglet," the compilers were apparently convinced that "Diego comes Porcelli" would be a better rendition. Since "Piglet" is no better a name for a county than for a count's father, however, they further assumed a spelling error. This produced the dignified, but apocryphal, "County of Portell."

46. The route in question was the great pilgrimage road to the shrine of Santiago de Compostela. This digression is taken directly from *De rebus Hispaniae* 5: 25, where it immediately precedes the account of King Sancho Garcés.

47. A recollection of the tumultuous period of Muslim attacks led by Al-manzor and his son Abd al-Malik from 977 to 1008. The tale that follows owes much to minstrel songs and is, for the most part, a paraphrase of *De rebus Hispaniae* 5: 26. The Aragonese based their claim of right of independence from Navarre and for the legitimacy of the ruling dynasty of Aragon established by Ramiro on these legendary and romanticized events.

48. There is a certain parallel to the tale of Arthur and Guinevere at this point. Sancho's wife has been accused of adultery by his eldest son, and one or the other of them must suffer death. Sancho cannot decide the matter according to his own wishes, since he has brought his realms under the rule of law. In Arthur's case, this dilemma eventually led to the disintegration of his realm. The same is true in the case of Sancho el Mayor, and Aragon achieved independence in the process.

49. Sancho held Castile by right of his wife, and it might normally have passed to their eldest son. If Sancho were no longer to hold her as wife, however, the land would revert to her. The queen appears to have made the claim of reversion against García for failing to hold her in the respect proper to a mother, a nice legal point and one that, considering the circumstances, King Sancho could not refuse. Also, one might note that the brothers had also defamed her counselor, presumably a leading Castilian noble, and the queen had no power to forgive her son this insult.

50. At the time, Castile was still only a county. Fernando did not assume a royal title until his accession to the crown of Leon by right of his wife, 22 June 1038.

51. It was the custom of the Navarrese and Aragonese to endow their brides with property called an *arras* to serve as security for the wife's proper treatment. Should the husband deal unjustly with her, or fail to accord her due respect, the *arras* would revert to her full possession. It would seem that this, too, was part of the queen's price for pardoning García.

52. One of the documents recording these arrangements, Sancho's donation to Ramiro, has been preserved and published as *CSJP* no. 66, dated (1035?).

53. Benedictines, so called from their customary black robes. The traditional date for this reform is 21 April 1025, but is based more on legend than fact. The Benedictine establishment actually took place in 1071, under the direction of King Sancho Ramírez of Aragon (1064–1094), and marked the formal foundation of the monastery of San Juan de la Peña, on the location of the primitive, and perhaps abandoned, monastery of Saints Julián and Basilissa.

54. Sancho actually died in October 1035 and was buried in the monastery of San Salvador de Oña.

55. In the writing of Chapters 16 through 20, the compilers utilized as a base text the early fourteenth-century Aragonese chronicle known as the *Crónica de los*

estados peninsulares. This has been edited by Antonio Ubieto Arteta (Granada: Universidad de Granada, 1955). The compilers elaborated their account from various other sources. Local traditions, *cantares de gesta*, and minstrel tales influence this entire section of the *Chronicle*. The result is an often inseparable mixture of history and romance.

56. Gonzalo was assassinated on 26 June 1043.

57. There were other reasons. See Lynn H. Nelson, "The Aragonese Acquisition of Sobrarbe and Ribagorza," *Estudios en homenaje a don Claudio Sánchez Albornoz en sus 90 años* 2 (Buenos Aires: Instituto de Historia de España, 1983): 227–236.

58. Gisberga had taken the name of her aunt, Ermisenda, the redoubtable countess of Barcelona, in whose court she had been reared, and who had probably arranged her marriage to Ramiro.

59. Sancha in fact married Ermengol III, count of Urgell (1040–1065), sometime about 1058. There is no record of Teresa having married at all.

60. This testament may be found in *CSJP* no. 159, dated 15 March 1061.

61. This was hardly the case. Ramiro appears to have conducted only one successful campaign against the Moors, that of 1058, in which he conquered the district of Benabarre.

62. Sancho de Peñalén (1054–1076).

63. These districts had in fact been reserved for the king of Navarre by the terms of Sancho el Mayor's testament, noted above. The text of the pact between Ramiro and Sancho of Navarre may be found in *CSJP* no. 172, dated (1063–1064), but probably closer to 1054. The actual case would appear to have been that Ramiro pledged aid to the young Sancho de Peñalén after the Navarrese defeat and death of King García in battle against the Castilians and Leonese at Atapuerca (1054). The pact was one in which Ramiro was given lands by King Sancho in exchange for his protection of the Navarrese against further territorial inroads by the Castilians and Leonese, and not from fear of the Muslims. The obscuring of the motives for the treaty of alliance and the reversal of the power relationship involved both suggest that this account was drawn from a Navarrese source.

64. This date has been much in dispute. It is far more likely to have been 1064.

65. Sancho of Castile was Ramiro's nephew.

66. This is a later and romanticized account. A contemporary and detailed Muslim narrative states that Ramiro was killed by a Muslim warrior who managed to infiltrate the Christian camp. Castilian troops, if present at all, played a negligible role in the affair.

67. There is little data on the so-called War of the Three Sanchos. The conflict apparently took place in the summer of 1064, and the Castilians may have made some territorial gains in the course of the hostilities. A curious aspect of the account provided by the *Chronicle* is the description of the disgraceful flight of the king of Castile upon a horse equipped only with a halter. This was precisely the same act ascribed by Navarrese chroniclers to Ramiro of Aragon in his defeat by the Navarrese at Tafalla (late 1035 or early 1036). See the *Historia Silense*, ed. Justo Pérez de Urbel and Atiliano González Ruíz-Zorilla (Madrid: CSIC, 1959), pp. 180–181.

68. At this time, Huesca was in fact subordinate to the Muslim kingdom of Zaragoza, the ruler of which was Ahmad ibn Suleiman al-Muqtadir.

69. Felicia was the daughter of the influential and well-connected French noble, Hilduin of Roucy. Their French relatives would later provide good service to Sancho's sons, Pedro, Alfonso, and Ramiro.

70. Actually from 1064 to 1076, or twelve years.

71. Wednesday, 22 March 1071. The Roman liturgy replaced the Visigothic, or Toledan, rite. The standardization of church liturgy was an important aspect of the Gregorian reform, and Sancho's imposition of it in San Juan de la Peña marked his increasingly close relationship with the papacy. The Visigothic rite was restored on a limited basis in the cathedral of Toledo by Cardinal Francisco Jiménez de Cisneros and is still practiced there.

72. The form and wording of the following passages strongly suggest that the compilers were utilizing a set of annals maintained at San Juan de la Peña. Unfortunately, this source has not survived.

73. Thursday, 5 April 1084. The translation of saints' relics was a particularly solemn event, especially since the acquisition of additional relics increased the prestige and stature of the monastery considerably.

74. The battle of Morella was actually an Aragonese defeat in which a number of important persons fell captive to the Cid.

75. This may be one of two possible feast days, either the birth of Saint John, 24 June; or his martyrdom, 24 September. The first of these was a favorite day of celebration in medieval Spain.

76. Alfonso VI (1065–1109). For a biography of Alfonso, see Bernard F. Reilly, *The Kingdom of León-Castilla under King Alfonso VI: 1065–1109* (Princeton, NJ: Princeton University Press, 1988).

77. Sancho Ramírez constructed the castle-monastery of Montearagón a short distance northeast of the city. From this well-protected vantage point, Christian cavalry were able to interdict travel along the main route between Huesca and Lérida and to interrupt at will agricultural work throughout the fertile plain that surrounded the city. Huesca's prosperity was slowly destroyed by these tactics.

78. A curious phrase, suggesting that the dying king had prophetic powers.

79. 4 June 1094.

80. The present Pueyo de Sancho, a hill a short distance south of the city of Huesca. From this position, Pedro dominated the southern suburbs of the city, cut the inhabitants off from their country estates, and controlled traffic along the road from Zaragoza. Pedro did not in fact continue the siege of Huesca without interruption. He left in July 1094 to meet with the Cid near Valencia and spent the spring of 1095 capturing the Muslim positions of Naval and Salinas. It was not until May 1095, almost a year after the death of Sancho, that Pedro fortified Pueyo de Sancho and recommenced the siege.

81. Al-Musta'in II (1085–1110).

82. Altabas is on the northern outskirts of the city of Zaragoza; Zuera is some twenty kilometers to the north.

83. Almúdevar lies some fifteen kilometers southwest of Huesca.

84. The "great pilgrimage" was the First Crusade. The battle of Alcoraz took place on 19 November 1096, that of Antioch on 28 June 1098. The anachronism is evident, but the story illustrates the desire of the Aragonese to connect their

conquests with the crusading ideal. A chapel to Saint George, patron of the crusaders, was built on the Pueyo de Sancho, and King Pedro later built a fortress in the suburbs of Zaragoza to which he gave the name Juslibol, or "Deus lo vult," the battle cry of the crusaders.

85. The *Crónica de los estados peninsulares*, upon which this passage is based, states that Fortún received his cognomen of Maza from the Romance word for "mace." The Mazas were in fact an important Aragonese family, with their seat in Huesca. In this Latin version of the story, where the word for "mace" is *clavus*, the point has been completely lost. An Aragonese author would not have made such a mistake, providing good evidence that these sections of the *Chronicle* were submitted to King Pedro in Aragonese and translated into Latin in Barcelona.

86. 26 November 1096. The triumphal entry into the city in fact occurred on 25 November 1096.

87. The Cid had not commended himself to Pedro. In November 1091, King Sancho Ramírez concluded a treaty of alliance with Rodrigo Díaz of Bivar, el Cid, and this pact was renewed by Pedro in 1094. The Aragonese had territorial ambitions in the coastal area around Castellón, and Aragonese troops had been operating in this region since at least 1093.

88. This event was the subject of a *cantar de gesta*, a version of which has been published by Carola Reig, *El Cantar de Sancho II y Cerco de Zamora* (Madrid: CSIC, 1947).

89. This statement is anachronistic. Pedro Rodríguez of Azagra held Albarracín from 1168 to 1186, more than seventy years after the events being discussed.

90. King Pedro received the Cid's messengers in January 1097.

91. The leader of the Muslim forces was Muhammad, nephew of Yusuf ibn Tashfin, founder of the Almoravid movement.

92. A copy of the document to which the compilers refer is preserved in the *Libro de San Voto*, a manuscript volume currently held by the Biblioteca de la Facultad de Derecho de la Universidad de Zaragoza. It is listed in Jaffe-Löwenfeld, *Regesta pontificum romanorum* (2d ed., 2 vols., Leipzig: Veit, 1885–1888) as no. 5562, and is considered by its editors to be a falsification. On the other hand, such a privilege would have been merely a confirmation of a grant made to Sancho Ramírez by Gregory VII. The text of this document has been published in *Colección diplomática de la Catedral de Huesca*, ed. Antonio Durán Gudiol (2 vols., Zaragoza: CSIC, 1965–1969), no. 38, dated 17 February 1074.

93. The date of 1125 for the death of Pedro's children, who predeceased him, is clearly an error. Pedro died in Bearne sometime between 27 and 30 September 1104.

94. The history of this remarkable woman and her troubled marriage is presented in Bernard F. Reilly's *The Kingdom of León-Castilla under Queen Urraca, 1109–1126* (Princeton: Princeton University Press, 1982).

95. Alfonso occupied the territories of Ejea and Tauste in 1105.

96. The *almogávares* were light-armed troops excelling in guerilla warfare and fighting in broken terrain. They were among the most effective fighting men in Europe during the later Middle Ages.

97. It should also be noted that Count Rotrou and King Alfonso were cousins.

98. This entire account is based upon a Navarrese fabrication designed to

justify their possession of Tudela. Count Rotrou of Perche did not participate in the siege of Zaragoza. See Lynn H. Nelson, "Rotrou of Perche and the Aragonese Conquest," *Traditio* 26 (1970): 113–133.

99. Zaragoza had in fact lost its independent and royal status in 1110 and had been ruled by Almoravid governors since that time. Abu Bakr, the last governor, died in late 1117, and a new governor had not yet been appointed when the city was invested. The leader of the Muslim forces outside the city was Abd-Allah ibn Mazdali, governor of Granada.

100. The siege lasted from 22 May to 18 December 1118.

101. The city consisted of four quarters: two Muslim, one Christian, and one Jewish. The Christian quarter was located in the area now dominated by the great cathedral-shrine of Nuestra Señora del Pilar.

102. The street still exists, with the same name: Conde de Alperche.

103. The battle of Cutanda was fought on 17 June 1120. Among the combatants was Duke William IX of Aquitaine (ruled 1087–1127), the first of the troubadours. Miramozmelim is actually not a proper name, but *amir al-muslimin*, meaning "ruler of the Muslims."

104. Much of this region was overrun in 1119 to 1120, but it was not secured until after the victory at Cutanda.

105. The troubles between Urraca and Alfonso had begun before, not after, the conquest of Zaragoza.

106. The Castilians recognized Urraca as the rightful lord of the lands of Leon-Castile. They held these lands as fiefs but had pledged homage to Alfonso and received them from his hands when he was Urraca's husband and lord. They could not hold lands of one lord and owe fealty to another. Since the ties of homage were between each individual and Alfonso, and could not be dissolved unless one broke faith with the other, their only recourse was to give up their lands.

107. The battle commander, who was often the king, traditionally led the last rank in the medieval Spanish order of battle.

108. The battle of Candespina took place on 26 October 1110.

109. Count Raymond was actually the son of the duke of Burgundy and brother of Henri, count of Portugal and husband of Urraca's illegitimate half-sister Teresa. "Raymond" was, however, a favorite name within the family of the counts of Toulouse, and the scribe's mistake an understandable one.

110. The battle of Viadongos probably occurred in October 1111.

111. Alfonso was crowned king of Galicia on 17 September 1111; Urraca ruled in Leon-Castile until her death in March 1126.

112. Sancho of Navarre (1054–1076) was in fact the son of García Sánchez III (1035–1054). The lands in question had actually been lost to Castile in the aftermath of the assassination of Sancho el de Peñalén in 1076.

113. The so-called Peace of Támara was concluded in July 1127. The statement that Castile had been held for Alfonso Raimúndez constitutes a recognition that Alfonso of Aragon had no legal claim to this territory, but justifies his occupation of these lands by asserting that he had held them as a quasi-regent during Alfonso Raimúndez's minority.

114. The battle took place at Anzul, near Lucena, 10 March 1126. The Granadan

army, reinforced by troops from Seville and a large force from Africa, was commanded by Abu-l-Tahir, governor of Granada.

115. Alfonso had begun the investment of Fraga as early as July 1133. Muslim forces did not assemble to attack the Christians until 17 July 1134. Although Alfonso's defeat was absolute and many of his leaders were killed, he himself managed to escape. He died some days later, 7 September 1134.

116. Alfonso has joined Roderigo, Frederick, Arthur, Sebastian and other legendary kings who sleep, waiting to awaken at their countries' hour of greatest need.

117. In 1175 a blacksmith who claimed to be the returned Alfonso el Batallador managed to convince several of the Aragonese leaders who interviewed him that he was telling the truth. He was hanged in 1181 by order of King Alfonso II.

118. Pedro of Atarés, also known as Pedro Taresa or Talesa (d. 1151), was the grandson of Count Sancho Ramírez, illegitimate son of Ramiro I. It is interesting to note that the Borgia family of Italy were among his descendants.

119. Perhaps because the site chosen for the assembly was his own lordship.

120. The text of this document has been published by José María Lacarra, "Documentos para el estudio de la reconquista y repoblación del valle del Ebro. Serie I," *Estudios de Edad Media de la Corona de Aragón* 2 (1946), no. 3, dtd. 3 May 1093.

121. The monastery of Sahagún, in the province of León. An account hostile to Ramiro may be found in the *Crónicas anónimas de Sahagún*, ed. Antonio Ubieto Arteta (Textos Medievales, no. 75, Zaragoza: Anubar, 1987).

122. Ramiro was never confirmed in any of the dignities. The death of his brother precluded his exercising any authority in Roda-Barbastro. Since about 1130, he had been acting as prior of the monastery of San Pedro el Viejo in Huesca.

123. In addition to providing for public hygiene, medieval baths were favorite places for assignations and prostitution. The porters of such an establishment had to be exceedingly discreet. This explains their refusal to disturb Pedro or to discuss his business with his Navarrese visitors.

124. Ladrón was count of Vizcaya, Guipúzcoa, and Alava, and brought the power of these territories to bear in his support of García.

125. Chapter 17 above contains no information about Ramiro's vengeance upon Ramón, who murdered their brother. Coupled with the annalistic form of part of this chapter, the lack of such data would seem to be conclusive evidence that the compilers were using annals of the reign of Sancho Ramírez which contained fuller information than they presented, and are now lost.

126. García was, in fact, the grandson of the Cid, being the son of the Cid's daughter, Christina.

127. The pope actually opposed the accession of both Ramiro Sánchez and García Ramírez. In his testament, Alfonso had left his realms to the Knights of the Holy Sepulcher, of the Hospital of the Poor, and of the Temple of Solomon. The accession of Ramiro and García nullified these donations, which the pope was anxious to preserve.

128. The entire account of the assemblies of Borja and Monzón is a fabrication. The Aragonese, with the citizens of Jaca and Huesca leading the way, called for

Ramiro's accession immediately after the death of Alfonso el Batallador. In the case of both the Aragonese and Navarrese, considerations of hereditary right appear to have been paramount.

129. Ramiro married Agnes of Poitiers at Jaca at the close of 1135. Agnes, sister of the late Duke William IX of Aquitaine, had been the widow of the viscount of Thouars since 1127.

130. It appears that there may have been an outright rebellion against Ramiro in October 1135. Centered upon a noble clique abetted by southern French magnates, it was quelled only after Ramiro's alliance with Count Ramón Berenguer IV of Barcelona. See Antonio Ubieto Arteta, "La campana de Huesca," *Revista de Filología Española* 35 (1951): 29–61.

131. As a monk and cleric, he could not easily advise Ramiro to start killing people.

132. A similar incident is recounted by Livy, I, 54.

133. There is some conflict between the statement that he had selected for decapitation only those who had behaved criminally toward him and the sentiment that he would have killed them all had he had the opportunity.

134. The romantic tale of the bell of Huesca has long been a favorite of the Aragonese. The room in which these events supposedly occurred is still shown in the Provincial Museum of Huesca, once the royal palace of the kings of Aragon.

135. The following passages, through the redemption of Caxal, appear to have been based upon an account preserved in San Juan de la Peña. The text of a document containing this narrative, and purporting to be a transcription made in 1293 of an old parchment in the archives of San Juan de la Peña, has been published by Prósper Bofarull Mascaró, *Colección de documentos inéditos del Archivo de la Corona de Aragon* (41 vols., Barcelona, 1847–1910) 4: 360–364. It is discussed by Charles J. Bishko, "A Hispano-Cluniac Benefactor in the Epoch of Navarro-Aragonese Separation: Fortún Garcés Cajal and the Founding of San Adrián de Vadoluengo (Sangüesa), 1133–1145," *Estudios en homenaje a don Claudio Sánchez Albornoz en sus 90 años* 2 (Buenos Aires: Instituto de Historia de España, 1983): 275–312.

136. The Pact of Vadoluengo was concluded in early January 1135.

137. No doubt referring to the document or documents in which Sancho el Mayor had demarcated the lands of Ramiro and García.

138. The other two were Pedro of Atarés and Ferriz of Santa Eulalia.

139. The sequence of events appears to have been reversed. Bishop Sancho paid King García considerable sums out of his treasury in July and August 1135, but Cajal was not taken prisoner until the summer of 1137.

140. King Alfonso VII's decision to switch support from García of Navarre to Ramiro of Aragon marked the turn of Ramiro's fortunes and allowed him to address internal difficulties within his kingdom. The *Chronicle* overstates Ramiro's position. Ramiro in fact did homage to Alfonso VII for the kingdom of Zaragoza in August 1136. In a concord of October 1136, it was agreed that Alfonso would retain the western half of the territory, including Calatayud, Soria, and Alagón.

141. Petronilla was born on 29 June 1136, and was betrothed at Barbastro in August 1137.

142. Margarita was in fact the niece of Count Rotrou of Perche. The count was childless.

143. Ramiro retired to the monastery-church of San Pedro el Viejo in Huesca.

144. Ramiro died 16 August 1157.

145. Chapters 22 through 32, discussing the counts of Barcelona, are based almost entirely on the *Gesta Comitum Barcinonensium*, which has been edited by L. Barrau-Dihigo and J. Massó Torrents (Barcelona: Institut d'Estudis Catalans, 1925). The origins and early growth of the country of Barcelona are discussed at length by Archibald R. Lewis, *The Development of Catalan and Southern French Culture* (Austin: University of Texas Press, 1965).

146. That is, Guifred had commended himself and pledged homage and fealty to the king.

147. Grabbing another's beard was a very grave insult among the medieval Spanish. *The Song of Cid* is replete with references to the pulling of beards.

148. Salomó of Cerdanya held the county of Barcelona from 864 to 873.

149. This episode, whether historical or legendary, was the basis of Catalan claims of independence from the king of France. Ramón d'Abadal i de Vinyals believes that King Louis gave the counties of Barcelona and Girona to Guifred as part of the arrangements concluded at the Council of Troyes, 11 September 878. See his *Els primers comtes catalans*, Biografies catalanes, 1 (Barcelona: Teide, 1958), p. 65.

150. The monastery of Ripoll is located in the mountains north of Vic and was reputed to be the oldest congregation in Catalan lands. It was to Ripoll that King Pedro sent for materials upon which to base this section of his history. The compilers at Ripoll, which was located near the old counties of Cerdanya and Besalú, sometimes confused the succession in those counties with that of Barcelona.

151. The four sons of Guifred I were, in fact: Guifred II Borrell, count of Barcelona (897–911); Sunyer, count of Barcelona (911–947); Sunifred II, count of Urgell (898–940); and Miró II, count of Cerdanya and Besalú (897–927).

152. The account has conflated Guifred I el Pilós (870–897) and his successor, Guifred II Borrell (897–911).

153. The chapter refers to Miró II the younger, who ruled in the counties of Cerdanya and Besalú (897–927). His brother Sunyer succeeded Guifred II Borrell in ruling the county of Barcelona (911–947).

154. Miró's sons were counts of Cerdanya and Besalú: Sunifred II, count of Cerdanya (927–967); Oliba Cabreta, count of Cerdanya (967–990); Guifred II, count of Besalú (927–957); and Miró III, count of Besalú (967–984) and bishop of Girona.

155. Sunifred II succeeded to the counties of Cerdanya (927–967) and Besalú (957–967). Borrell (947–992) and Miró (947–966), sons of Sunyer and grandsons of Guifred I, jointly succeeded Sunyer (911–947) in the county of Barcelona.

156. The count of Urgell was actually their great-uncle, Sunifred II (897–950).

157. Sunifred II, count of Cerdanya and Besalú, died in about 965.

158. The succession was actually much simpler. See note 155 above. Borrell was the son of Sunyer, not Sunifred II of Urgell, but also uncle of Sunifred II of Cerdanya and Besalú.

159. The reason for the compilers' difficulty is quite clear. Sunifred had not been

count of Barcelona, but of Cerdanya, and his brother, Oliba Cabreta, had succeeded him in that lordship (966–988). Borrell had succeeded to the county of Urgell upon the death of his uncle, Sunifred II, in 950, and held it until his death in 992.

160. The year was actually 985, when Almanzor's troops devastated the Catalan countryside and took and burned Barcelona. Another attack in 1002 also caused great damage.

161. Bernat I "Trencaferre," count of Besalú (990–1020); Guifred II, count of Cerdanya (990–1050). One of the great figures of his age, Oliba has been studied by Ramón d'Abadal i de Vinyals, *L'Abat Oliba, bisbe de Vic i la seva època* (3d ed., Barcelona: Editorial Aedos, 1962).

162. The expedition to Córdoba took place in 1010 at the invitation of one of the parties in the civil war that was destroying the unity of the Caliphate after the end of the military dictatorship of Almanzor and his sons. A second expedition was directed against Granada in 1018. Count Ramón Borrell was forced to retire from this operation and died a short time later.

163. Ramón Borrell died, actually aged forty-five, 25 February 1018.

164. The count was interred in the church of Santa Creu, in Barcelona; see Santiago Sobrequés Vidal, *Els grans comtes de Barcelona* (Barcelona: Editorial Vicens-Vives, 1961), p. 27 and n. 67. A sixteenth-century manuscript of the Aragonese version fills the lacuna with the name of the monstery of Ripoll, but it is untrustworthy, with many baseless additions and expansions.

165. Count Guifred of Cerdanya died in the year 1050. He had ruled Cerdanya for sixty years (990–1050).

166. "Minorisa" is Manresa. By Ramón Borrell's testament, Guillem was given the county of Ausona.

167. This unusually harsh appraisal is shared by other chroniclers and may have been based upon two factors: (a) Berenguer appears to have preferred peace to war, and (b) by the terms of his father's testament, he was forced to share power with a woman, his mother, the redoubtable Countess Ermisenda.

168. Berenguer Ramón died on 31 March 1035, before reaching the age of forty. The place of his burial is unknown, but he died in Barcelona and it would seem likely for him to have been interred, like his father, in the cathedral church of Santa Creu. The same defective manuscript of the Aragonese version of the *Chronicle* discussed in note 165 above, however, fills the lacuna with *desus dito monasterio*, referring to Ripoll.

169. By the time of Count Ramón Berenguer, Muslim Spain consisted of a number of independent *taifa* ("party") kingdoms, constantly squabbling among themselves and almost defenseless against the Christian kingdoms. It became the custom for these small states to pay regular retainers, or *parias*, to a Christian protector to guarantee themselves security from attack from their protector, assistance in the event of attack by another Christian power, and effective military aid in case they found themselves too hard-pressed by a Muslim neighbor. Ramón Berenguer was a consummate player of this game and managed to enrich himself and his county by securing large and numerous *parias*.

170. The traditional date given for this assembly is 1068, but the papal legate, Hugh Candidus, who was in Barcelona in 1064 and 1071, was not present in 1068.

171. He actually died in 1040.

172. The account conflates the rule of Ramón Guifred (1050–1068) and that of his son, Guillem Ramón (1068–1095).

173. Guillem Jordá, count of Cerdanya (1095–1109); Bernat Guillem, count of Cerdanya (1109–1117).

174. The marriage took place in the spring of 1078.

175. By the terms of the testament of their father, Ramón Berenguer II (1076–1082) and Berenguer Ramón II (1076–1096) ruled jointly, an arrangement similar to that of counts Borrell and Miró during the period from 947 to 966. This situation suited neither brother, and they were constantly at odds.

176. The assassination occurred on 5 December 1082.

177. Although it was generally accepted that Berenguer Ramón had planned and directed his brother's murder, no conclusive proof was ever brought forward. For this reason, he continued to rule for another fourteen years, to 1096.

178. Although the circumstances of his death are unknown, it has been conjectured that Berenguer Ramón joined the crusading forces of Raymond of Toulouse and died before the walls of Jerusalem on 20 June 1099. See Santiago Sobrequés Vidal, *Els grans comtes de Barcelona,* Biografies catalanes, 2 (Barcelona: Editorial Vicens-Vives, 1961), p. 149.

179. Berenguer Ramón accepted Ramón Berenguer III as ward and heir on 18 June 1086, and the lad began appearing with the title of count in documents as early as 1089.

180. Gilbert of Geraudan (1100–1112).

181. He ruled Provence from 1112 to 1131.

182. In 1128, Alfonso VII of Leon-Castile married Berenguera, one of Ramón Berenguer's daughters by his third marriage.

183. A Pisan-Catalan expedition seized Mallorca in 1114, a feat memorialized in an epic poem, the *Liber Maiolichinus de gestis pisanorum illustribus.* The island was retaken by the Almoravids in late 1115 or early 1116.

184. The county of Tripoli, in present-day Lebanon.

185. The compilers are perhaps confusing the duration of Bernat III's rule with that of Bernat II (1066–1100), which lasted thirty-four years.

186. See chapter 20 above for a more detailed account.

187. The siege of Almería took place from 1 August to 17 October 1147.

188. The passage is rather chauvinistic. The capture of Almería was the work of Alfonso VII of Leon-Castile.

189. Tortosa surrendered on 31 December 1148 after a siege of six months. The enterprise had been granted the status of a crusade by Pope Eugenius III.

190. Lérida and Fraga capitulated on the same day, 24 October 1149. Miravet, Ciurana, and other districts along the Ebro were conquered between 1152 and 1153.

191. Berenguer Ramón was killed in 1144. The pirates involved were probably Genoese sea-raiders

192. The viscounts of Baux, encouraged by the count of Toulouse and Emperor Frederick I, opposed the rule of the house of Barcelona for some time. The family offered submission to Ramón Berenguer in September 1150 after the death of

Raymond of Baux, but Raymond's son, Hugh, rebelled against Ramón in 1153 and again in 1160.

193. Frederick Barbarossa abandoned Hugh of Baux to his fate, and Ramón Berenguer and his nephew acknowledged that they held the marquisate of Provence and the city of Arles in fief from the Holy Roman Emperor.

194. Ramón was in fact forty-seven when he died on 6 August 1162. He had journeyed to Turin to confer with the Emperor Frederick, who was trying to enlist his support for the anti-pope the emperor had established.

195. Count Ramón Berenguer IV soon gained a saintly reputation among the populace. This poetic passage is echoed in other sources of the time. Ramón became a figure of inspiration for poets, troubadours, and minstrels.

196. Although the exact date has been a matter of considerable discussion, it now appears that Alfonso was born between 1 and 25 March 1157. See Jordi Ventura, *Alfons 'el Cast'. El primer comte rei* (Barcelona: Editorial Aedos, 1961), pp. 53–59.

197. Ramón Berenguer acted as regent from 1162 to 1164.

198. Although Alfonso was proclaimed count of Barcelona in 1163 and king of Aragon in 1164, he did not reach his majority until age sixteen, in 1173. The reins of government during the intervening years appear to have been in the hands of the seneschal of Barcelona, Guillem of Montcada, and Guillem Torroja.

199. See chapter 20 above.

200. Cuenca capitulated on 14 September 1177.

201. The negotiations between Alfonso II of Aragon and Alfonso VII of Castile took place in August 1177. Part of the price paid for the return of the lands of Zaragoza was the cession of Murcia to Castile, an act for which Alfonso II has sometimes been condemned. The important gain, however, was that Aragon was released from all ties of homage to Castile. With this, Aragon finally reemerged as an equal and independent power in the Peninsula. The reason the compilers do not make a bigger point of this achievement is because they have consistently refused to admit that Aragon had at any time owed homage to Castile.

202. The marriage was celebrated at Zaragoza on 18 January 1174. The Royal Monastery of Sigena, in the province of Huesca, was authorized as a convent by the Hospitallers and given a rule on 6 October 1188.

203. Teruel was repopulated in October 1174. Guiraut II, count of Rosselló (1164–1178), had left the county to Alfonso by his testament of 1172, the text of which may be found in the *Liber Feudorum Maior*, ed. F. Miquel Rosell (2 vols., Barcelona: CSIC, 1955–1957), no. 792, dtd. 4 July 1172. Guiraut died in 1178, and Alfonso united Rosselló to his other realms.

204. The castle of Albaron.

205. With this act, the family of Baux finally transferred their allegiance from the counts of Toulouse to the house of Barcelona, to which the family remained loyal. The nobles of Provence swore their allegiance to Alfonso in the city of Arles on 16 August 1167.

206. Alfonso met with Richard I at Najac de Roergue on 14 April 1185, and the two formed an alliance against the count of Toulouse. The expedition through the lands of Toulouse that followed was a joint Anglo-Aquitanian-Aragonese venture.

207. The date of this battle is not fixed with any certainty, but it has traditionally been thought to have taken place in 1191.

208. Constanza's first marriage was to Emmerich, king of Hungary (1196–1204). Her second match was with Frederick II Hohenstaufen, Holy Roman Emperor (1212–1250), king of Two Sicilies, and king of Jerusalem.

209. Eleanora married Raymond VI, count of Toulouse, and Sancha married Raymond VII, his son and successor. A fourth daughter, Dulce, was a nun in the convent of Sigena.

210. Alfonso's pilgrimage lasted from August 1195 to early March 1196.

211. Numerous writers refer to a general famine throughout Europe that persisted, with greater or lesser severity, through the years 1195 and 1196.

212. This interpolation is due to the compilers' attempt to continue to note the affairs of the county of Urgell.

213. The exact date of his death was 25 April 1196.

214. King Pedro II died in battle, supporting vassals of his who had opposed northern French forces called in by Pope Innocent III to eliminate the Albigensian heretics. He was thus open to charges of having supported the heresy, and the *Chronicle* is at pains to defend him from such accusations.

215. Other sources make the same complaint against Pedro; he taxed his realms heavily, his economic policies were ruinous, he was always short of money, and he left his son and heir heavily in debt.

216. See notes 208 and 209 above.

217. Pedro married Marie of Montpellier on 15 June 1204. She was the daughter of Guillaume VIII and Eudoxia Comnenus, daughter of Manuel Comnenus, emperor of Constantinople (1143–1180).

218. The pilgrimage took place in November 1204. It has been suggested that Pedro's primary motive in visiting Rome was to place his lands under papal protection during the suppression of the Albigensian heresy to which Innocent III had committed himself.

219. This coronation took place on 11 November 1204.

220. See note 92 above.

221. Ibid.

222. The town of Montpellier rebelled against Pedro's arbitrary rule, and he was forced to agree to a negotiated peace on 22 October 1206.

223. The factors troubling the marriage were many. Pedro wished to annul the union in order to marry Marie of Montferrat, heiress to the kingdom of Jerusalem. After their wedding, he had avoided consummating the marriage, avoiding his wife and insofar as possible, refusing even to see her. The leaders of Montpellier made continued efforts to reconcile the couple. Meanwhile, Pedro openly kept a mistress in the town, to his wife's humiliation. Jaime, Pedro's heir and successor, was conceived during a brief reconciliation in early May 1207. This gave rise to the popular romance that Marie had gained the assistance of Pedro's maid and valet and, in a darkened bedchamber, had posed as the king's mistress in order to provide the realm with a legitimate heir. A similar tale is told by Boccaccio.

224. Innocent III rejected Pedro's petition for an annulment on 19 January 1213.

225. Marie of Montpellier died in Rome on 21 April 1213. It was believed that scrapings from her tomb, when drunk with wine or water, could cure illness.

226. The battle of Alarcos took place on 19 July 1195.

227. Peace was restored with Navarre by the treaties of Monteagudo (1208) and Mallén (1209), the conclusion of which was made possible by the payment by King Sancho the Strong of twenty thousand *morabetines* to King Pedro.

228. The temporary occupation of Ubeda was one of the lesser operations following the great Christian victory of Las Navas de Tolosa, 16 July 1212. The compilers have reversed the order of events.

229. Castilian, Portuguese, Navarrese, Aragonese, and Catalan troops all contributed to this signal victory, which was certainly not Pedro's personal and individual achievement. After Las Navas de Tolosa, the Muslims never again posed a serious threat to Christian Spain.

230. Ermengol VIII died in 1208, and Guiraut of Cabrera, husband of Ermengol's sister, seized power. The widowed countess and her daughter, Aurembaix, placed themselves under Pedro's protection. Pedro betrothed Aurembaix to his son, Jaime.

231. This narrative owes much to *De rebus Hispaniae* 6: 4, with the exception that the compilers fail to mention that the Catalans also deserted King Pedro.

232. Arnau of Narbonne had been directed by the pope on 15 January 1213 to work with King Pedro in attempting to compose affairs in the region. See A. Potthast, *Regesta pontificum romanorum* (2 vols., Berlin, 1874–1875), no. 4648.

233. The fact that the compilers provide two accounts of the battle of Muret is a sign of an imperfect redaction.

234. The customs of France would have guaranteed the lives of the besieged, since they would have surrendered before their walls had been breached. Spanish customs offered no such guarantee. This second account of the preliminaries of the battle of Muret is that presented in the autobiography of Pedro's son, King Jaime.

235. The besiegers' discipline seems to have been lax. Pedro's son Jaime, who was an eyewitness, wrote that his father had spent the preceding night in such strenuous entertainment that he was unable to stand up for the reading of the Gospel at the next morning's mass.

236. The battle took place on 13 September 1213.

237. This would appear to be considerably in error. Pedro was born sometime around 1177 and would thus have been about thirty-seven at the time of his death.

238. It was not until February 1217 that Pope Honorius allowed Pedro's body to be taken to his chosen resting place. The corpses of Pedro and five of his Aragonese supporters were brought from France and interred at Sigena on 30 September 1217.

239. The reign of King Jaime is illuminated by his autobiography, the remarkable *Chronicle of James I, King of Aragon*, trans. John Forster (2 vols., London: Chapman and Hall, 1883).

240. Jaime was born on 2 February 1208, and was thus five and a half years of age at his father's death. He is better known by the sobriquet "the Conqueror."

241. Jaime was taken from his mother by King Pedro on 27 January 1211, and turned over to Simon of Montfort as a surety of friendship between the two.

242. It would appear that the same qualities that made Fernando a poor abbot

convinced many that he would be a good king. The Aragonese nobility feared possible attacks by Castile during the long minority of Jaime. The populace, on the other hand, feared a war of succession.

243. Simon relinquished Jaime, probably in May 1214, at Narbonne.

244. Sancho was the son of Ramón Berenguer IV, count of Barcelona.

245. This complex arrangement was ratified by a papal bull of 23 January 1216.

246. The knighting took place shortly after his marriage to Eleanora in 1220.

247. The compilers devote little attention to the rebellions and other disturbances that plagued the realms, particularly Aragon, during Jaime's early years. There is a disinclination throughout the *Chronicle* to dwell upon challenges to royal power.

248. The moral set by the compilers is hardly pertinent to the actual events. In 1226, Pedro Ahones wished to invade the lands of a Muslim ruler with whom Jaime had concluded a treaty, and he refused to accept Jaime's denial of permission. There was a violent quarrel between the two, and Pedro attempted to draw his sword against the king. He was stopped in this act, the penalty for which could be death. Pedro then fled possible retribution, but was pursued and killed. His death sparked a widespread uprising throughout Aragon that was not composed until the spring of 1227.

249. The marriage was celebrated at Tarazona in 1220, when Jaime was thirteen years old.

250. Jaime and Eleanora had Alfonso VII of Castile as a common great-grandfather. The divorce was ratified by an ecclesiastical council meeting at Tarazona on 29 April 1229.

251. Violant, or Yolanda, was the daughter of Andrea II, king of Hungary (1205–1235), and niece on her mother's side of Pierre of Courtenay, emperor of Constantinople (1215–1219). The wedding took place near the close of 1235, probably at Barcelona.

252. See note 268, below.

253. Alfonso X "el Sabio," king of Leon and Castile (1252–1284).

254. This assembly, or *corts*, was held in Barcelona in December 1228. Not mentioned by the compilers as among Jaime's motives was his need to obtain the levy of a tax to finance the expedition.

255. This was in fulfillment of an oath recorded by the chronicler Bernat Desclot. The Muslim king died soon afterward.

256. The Muslims of Menorca began paying tribute in 1232. The Christians did not occupy the island until 1286, in the reign of Alfonso III.

257. Operations against Valencia began in 1232, when Pope Gregory IX granted its conquest the status of a crusade, and Jaime and his men took the customary crusader oath. The serious attack upon the city commenced after Jaime renewed his oath and an assembly celebrated at Monzón in October 1236 established a new tax in Aragon.

258. Murcia capitulated in January 1266.

259. The conquest of Murcia had in fact been conceded to Castile in 1179 by Alfonso II in exchange for Aragon's release from the homage rendered to Castile for the kingdom of Zaragoza. This agreement had been renewed in the treaty of Almizra, 26 March 1244.

260. Pedro of Portugal was granted Mallorca in 1231, in exchange for which he ceded the county of Urgell to Jaime. Urgell had come to Pedro through his marriage to Countess Aurembaix.

261. Jaime was in Lyon from 1 to 21 May 1274. The pope was present in fact to encourage Jaime to undertake a crusade, an attempt that failed.

262. Although Jaime proclaimed himself prepared to undertake the venture, the pope was unable to enlist sufficient support among the other leaders attending the council to make the venture worthwhile in Jaime's estimation.

263. Jaime had proposed partitioning his realms a number of times. The arrangement referred to here was agreed upon in 1262 and was repeated in later documents.

264. Sainte-Marie de Vauvert, near Montpellier.

265. This ceremony took place on 21 July 1276.

266. This address took place before a number of barons, knights, and burgesses of the realms.

267. Jaime abdicated on 21 July 1276 and died six days later at Valencia.

268. The invasion of Abu Yusuf, emir of Morocco, occurred in May 1275. Nuño González of Lara was killed in the Christian defeat at Ecija, 7 September 1275, and Archbishop Sancho was killed near Jaén the following October.

269. For a full biography of Pedro, see Ferran Soldevila, *Vida de Pere el Gran i d'Alfons el Liberal* (Barcelona: Editorial Aedos, 1963). Much of the period is covered by the contemporary *Crònica* of Bernat Desclot.

270. This account refers to the siege of 1266.

271. The Muslim rebellion broke out in 1275, and the Templars' defeat occurred in late June 1276.

272. Montesa fell on 29 September 1277. The compilers have pursued the rebellion of al-Azraq to its conclusion, rather than following a strictly chronological organization.

273. The coronation was celebrated on 17 November 1276.

274. This concord, reached in the Dominican monastery at Perpignan on 20 January 1278, was the result of a long dispute. King Jaime accepted his lands as fiefs of honor, pledging himself and his heirs to do homage to Pedro and his heirs. This homage carried with it the mutual obligation to render aid when needed. Pedro had representatives of Perpignan swear to withdraw their allegiance to Jaime if he failed to observe the terms of the concord.

275. Actually, Fernando de la Cerda had died in 1275. His widow, Blanche (sister of Philip III of France), supported by Queen Violant, wished King Alfonso X of Castile to designate her son, Alfonso de la Cerda, as heir. Alfonso refused, preferring to name his second son, Sancho, as heir. Blanche, Violant, and Alfonso de la Cerda sought refuge in Pedro's court while Blanche sought aid from her brother.

276. These events were part of a widespread unrest among the Catalan nobles in 1278.

277. The nobles claimed as their grievance in the uprising of 1280 that the king had refused to convene an assembly at Barcelona and confirm their traditional liberties.

278. The siege of Balaguer ended on 11 July 1280.

279. This conference took place at Toulouse, around 18 to 22 January 1281, and related to the failure of King Jaume of Mallorca to respect some of the terms of their concord of 1278.

280. Pedro's Mediterranean policy forms an essential element in Steven Runciman's *The Sicilian Vespers. A History of the Mediterranean World in the later Thirteenth Century* (Cambridge: Cambridge University Press, 1958).

281. Pedro embarked on 6 June 1282. The Sicilians' revolt against their French garrisons, known as the Sicilian Vespers, had taken place on 30 March, and Pedro was already considering intervening in the island's affairs.

282. Collo, in modern Algeria.

283. Pedro's ambassadors met with Pope Martin at Montefiascone in early August 1282. Martin already suspected that Pedro's fleet and army were really intended for Sicily, against the pope's French kinsmen. Pedro's request for crusader indulgences placed the pope in a difficult position.

284. The public beheading of the sixteen-year old Conrad of Hohenstaufen took place at Naples on 29 October 1268. The execution and the sham trial preceding it repelled many Europeans and permanently blackened the reputation of Charles of Anjou.

285. Pedro's right to Sicily was through his wife, Constanza, daughter of King Manfred of Sicily (1258–1266).

286. It was an instance of just this sort that had ignited the massacre of the French.

287. The Aragonese fleet landed at Trapani on 30 August 1282.

288. This is probably something of an exaggeration. Trapani lies some eighty kilometers from Palermo. Pedro entered Palermo on 4 September.

289. Pedro did not in fact enter Messina until 2 October 1282, more than a month after landing in Sicily.

290. Charles had, in fact, retired from Messina in late September, before Pedro's arrival at the city.

291. Aragonese troops entered Calabria in January 1283.

292. Edward I (1272–1307).

293. The day agreed upon was 1 June 1283.

294. Pedro left Sicily on 6 May 1283, landing at Cullera on 17 May and leaving little time for him to prepare for the scheduled tournament.

295. Edward of England had not agreed to sponsor the tournament and had not ordered his seneschal, Jean d'Agrilly, to make the field safe for Pedro by excluding French troops from the vicinity.

296. Pedro was issuing documents from Logroño on 10 June. Despite its romantic character, the incident of the tournament is attested by other sources and appears to have been an historical fact.

297. The siege was opened in mid-April 1284. Albarracín capitulated on 18 September and was occupied on 29 September. Pedro Nuñez of Lara had allied himself with the king of France, whose troops threatened Pedro's frontiers during the course of the siege.

298. Charles of Anjou died on 7 January 1285, after the siege had been completed.

299. Pedro was in Tarazona from 24 October to 1 November 1284, joining a Catalan force he had dispatched to the region in August under the command of Prince Alfonso.

300. King Pedro apparently had exiled Pedro Martínez of Bolea.

301. The expedition to Perpignan took place from 23 to 27 April 1285.

302. This blanket offer was made on 27 August 1283, some time before the actual attack began.

303. Charles's investiture at the hands of a papal legate took place in Paris on 27 February 1284.

304. Pedro occupied the pass of Panissars on 7 May 1285.

305. The French bypassed Pedro's army at Panissars and entered Catalunya through the pass of Maçana during the night of 8–9 June.

306. Pedro abandoned his position at Panissars on 12 June, after holding his men there for over a month.

307. Many of the inhabitants of Ampurias undertook guerilla operations against the French garrisons in the county, practicing the kind of warfare that their descendants would wage against Napoleon's troops five hundred years later.

308. Roger de Lauria and his fleet arrived at Barcelona on 23 August and his victory over the French fleet took place shortly afterward.

309. The compilers have backtracked here to late June to narrate the actions on land.

310. The battle of Santa María d'Agost, fought in mid-August 1285, was scarcely a Catalan victory, and the compilers studiously avoid discussing its outcome.

311. Pedro had promised the French king and his immediate followers that they would not be attacked. Lesser members of the crusading army enjoyed no such security.

312. The attacks on the retreating French were concentrated on 30 September and 1 October 1285.

313. Philip III died on 6 October 1285, of the same plague that had devastated his army and frustrated his plans.

314. Robert of Anjou was actually king of Naples (1309–1343).

315. The fleet sailed sometime in early November 1285. News of his father's death reached Alfonso on 17 November, and the city of Mallorca capitulated two days later.

316. Pedro died during the night of 10–11 November 1285.

317. The coronation was celebrated in April 1296, with rituals and ceremonies that set the standard for the coronations of later kings of the Crown of Aragon.

318. That is, the Aragonese forced this concession from him, rather than his having given it of his own free will.

319. King Alfonso III swore to the Privilege of the Union on 28 December 1287. Among other things, he agreed not to proceed against a member of the union without the permission of the Chief Justiciar and the *cortes*; that he would call a *cortes* at Zaragoza every November; that the *cortes* could assign to him advisors on Aragonese, Valencian, and Ribagorzan affairs; and that the *cortes* could depose him and elect another king if it wished, Meanwhile, he was to turn over royal castles and hostages to the Aragonese, who seemed bent on establishing a constitutional monarchy.

320. The conquest of Menorca took place in January 1287. The Muslim inhabitants were expelled from the island, many of them being sold into slavery.

321. Alfonso de la Cerda.

322. This took place in September 1288. By supporting the Infantes de la Cerda, Alfonso posed a threat to King Sancho of Castile. Aragon was still faced by powerful enemies, and this neutralized one, at least for a time.

323. The allies' invasion of Castile took place in mid-1289, after Alfonso de la Cerda had made a secret agreement to turn over Murcia to Alfonso of Aragon should he gain the throne of Castile.

324. Although King Edward betrothed his daughter to King Alfonso in 1282, he refused to release her to the Aragonese monarch or to pay him the dowry agreed upon. This gave him considerable power over Alfonso, who needed powerful friends, lacked money, and had not produced an heir.

325. The compilers obscure what really had happened. King Sancho of Castile and King Philip of France had made an alliance in June 1288, to which Alfonso had replied by having Alfonso de la Cerda acclaimed king in September 1288 and sending his defiance to Sancho. After securing a secret promise from Alfonso de la Cerda to cede Murcia to Aragon if he should gain the Castilian throne, Alfonso invaded Castile in the summer of 1289. Philip came to Sancho's aid by backing Jaume of Mallorca in an invasion of Catalunya and sending French troops through Navarre to invade Aragon. Alfonso of Aragon withdrew because his opponents would not allow him to attack them one by one, and Edward of England, his only potential ally, refused to commit himself in Alfonso's support.

326. The meeting to which the compilers are referring was that of Olerón, held in 1287. Although there were many diplomatic meetings between Aragonese representatives and those of other powers in the attempt to find a basis for peace, Alfonso personally attended only Olerón in 1287 and Canfranc in October of 1288.

327. Peace terms were finally arranged at a conference at Tarascon in February 1291. Alfonso's death some four months later prevented their implementation.

328. King Alfonso had developed a tumor in his thigh. This had abscessed, causing a fatal infection.

329. Alfonso died on 18 June 1291.

330. His marriage with Eleanor was never consummated.

331. Jaime landed at Barcelona on 13 August 1291. A standard biography of this monarch is that included in J. E. Martínez Ferrando, *Jaime II o el seny català. Alfons el Benigne* (2d ed., Barcelona: Editorial Aedos, 1963).

332. The *cortes* were held in November of 1291, in accordance with the union's demand that a *cortes* be convened in Zaragoza every November. See note 319 above.

333. The marriage with the eight-year-old princess María was arranged in a meeting at Monteagudo on 29 November 1291, and a civil ceremony was performed at Soria on 1 December.

334. The abortive conference at Logroño was held at the end of July 1293.

335. The marriage between Alfonso and Blanche of Anjou, which appears to have been a love match, was celebrated at Vilabertrán on 25 October 1295.

336. The preceding paragraph interrupts the flow of the narrative somewhat. The "project" referred to is Charles's frustrated plan to take King Jaime captive.

337. The conference was held at la Junquera in 1293.

338. This agreement, the Treaty of Anagni, was proclaimed by Pope Boniface VIII on 24 June 1295. The provisions included that Jaime would relinquish his claim to Sicily and return Mallorca to his uncle, Jaume. In exchange, the pope would confirm him in Aragon, lift the interdict in the Crown of Aragon, and grant him Sardinia and Corsica.

339. As noted above, the marriage of the twelve-year-old Blanche took place on 25 October. The compiler is in error on the date of the parties' arrival at Vilabertrán.

340. Federico did, however, accept the title "Lord of the Island" on 11 December 1295.

341. Federico was crowned at Palermo, 25 May 1296.

342. Jaime arrived in Rome in late March 1297.

343. These titles and obligations had been announced in the bull *Redemptor mundi*, 20 January 1297.

344. These concessions were announced in the bull *Super reges et regna*, 4 April 1297.

345. The fact that Fernando IV was a ten-year-old minor facilitated this unrest. Jaime took the lead in forming an alliance, which included Muhammad II of Granada, aimed at dismembering Castile. The allied invasion was launched in 1296.

346. The royal expedition against Murcia had ended by the beginning of August 1296.

347. The point would seem to be that Jaime's followers pleaded with the king to avoid battle in order to spare them the duty of trying to kill their kinsmen. Jaime, by pretending that their hesitation was based upon an apprehension of defeat, refused to recognize their dilemma. At this, a large number abandoned their ships in full view of the king.

348. . . . *in ruppibus tamen pictibus situata*. The Catalan version of the *Chronicle* speaks simply of stone forts.

349. The compilers have conflated two events. King Jaime restored Murcia to Castile in 1304 in accordance with the decision of a board of arbitration headed by King Dinis of Portugal. Jaime and Fernando IV of Castile concluded their alliance against the king of Granada at Alcalá de Henares in December 1308.

350. These operations were begun in late July 1309.

351. Fernando of Castile abandoned the siege of Algeciras in mid-January 1310.

352. Jaime's marriage to Marie of Lusignan, sister of Henri II of Cyprus (1285–1306), was celebrated in mid-September 1315. She died at Barcelona on 10 September 1322.

353. The fleet sailed on 23 May.

354. Alfonso left his supply vessels and other craft to catch up as best they could and used his galleys, which were not dependent on favorable winds, to reach Sardinia as quickly as possible.

355. The siege of Iglesia opened on 3 July 1323, and the city capitulated on 7 February 1324.

356. This battle, that of Lucocisterna, was waged against Pisan forces and took place on 7 February 1324.

357. The sally took place in April 1324.

358. This agreement was reached on 19 June 1324.

359. Teresa died at Zaragoza on 27 September 1327.

360. Later Pedro IV, "the Ceremonious" (1336–1387).

361. The king actually died on 2 November.

362. The coronation took place at Zaragoza, 2–4 April 1328. The *Chronicle* of Mutaner contains a famous description of the attendant formalities.

363. Alfonso's marriage to Eleanora was celebrated at Tarazona at the beginning of February 1329.

364. Pedro II (1337–1342).

Index

Abd al-Malik ibn Khatan, 5
Abd ar-Rahman
    III, caliph of Córdoba, 7
    king of Huesca, 19, 21
Abd ar-Rahman ibn Moncavia, 5
Abd ar-Rahman, king of Huesca, 6
Acumuer, 7
Adalmozaben, king of Zaragoza, 21
Ademuz, castle of, 59
Africa, 72, 96
Ager, viscounty of, 63, 103
Agnes, wife of Pedro I of Aragon, 25
Aibar, 11, 14, 17
Al-Azraq, 69
Alaric, Gothic king, 3
Alava, 5, 13, 58
Albanyo, castle of, 54
Albarracín, 24; castle of, 75; Fernando, lord
    of, 103; Pedro Fernández of Azagra,
    lord of, 61, 92; Pedro Rodríguez de
    Azagra, lord of, 24
Alcázar, 30
Alcira, 66
Alcira de Alfadra (Algeciras), siege of, 96
Alcoraz, battle of, 22, 23
Alcoyll, castle of, 71; church of Saint Peter
    of, 72
Alesves, 39
Alfonso
    I, king of Aragon, 19, 20, 22, 24, 25, 29–31,
        33, 37, 38
    II, king of the Crown of Aragon, 40, 51–
        56
    III, king of the Crown of Aragon, 62, 73,
        84–89, 102
    IV, king of the Crown of Aragon, 93, 97,
        100, 102
    VI, king of Castile, 20, 23–25, 27, 28
    VII, king of Castile, 28, 30, 33, 37–40, 49,
        51, 53

    VIII, king of Castile, 53, 54, 58, 59
    X, king of Castile, 62, 63, 65, 70
    IV, king of Leon, 12
    II, count of Provence, 55, 58
Alfonso de la Cerda, 87, 92
Alicante, 96
All-Saints, feast of, 91
Almazán, settlement of, 25
Almenar, conquest of, 20
Almería, 19, 30; conquest of, 51; siege of, 96
Almetzalem, king of Zaragoza, 26
Almodis, wife of Ramón Berenguer I, 47
Almogávars, 26
Almohades, arrival of, 68
Almoravids, arrival of, 24
Almúdevar, 23
Alphonse, count of Poitiers, 57
Altabas, 22
Alvaro, viscount of Ager, 71
Alvaro (Ermengol) IX, count of Urgell, 63
Alvarono, son of Ermengol IX of Urgell, 63
Ampurias, count of, 83, 88; county of, 80, 82
Antioch, battle of, 23
Apulia, 49
Aragon, invasion of, 75; house of, 60, 101;
    kingdom of, 102, 103
Aragón, river, 76
Aragonese Union, 84, 86, 102, 103
Arborea, judge of, 99
Arbués, 76
Arcaz, castle of, 50
Arga, 39
Argüedas, conquest of, 20
Arian heresy, 3
Arinzol, battle of, 30
Ariza, 38
Arles, 4, 54; archbishop of, 90; devastation
    of, 52
Armentera, siege of, 63
Arnaldo of Cabrera, 80

Arnau, archbishop of Narbonne, 59; bishop of Vic, 46
Arrian, 41
Artieda, 5
Ash Wednesday, 100
Astorga, 29
Asturias, 5, 13
Atarés, 7
Athaulf, Gothic king, 3
Aurembaix, countess of Urgell, 63
Ausonia (Vic), 2
Austria, duke of, 57
Avetito, donation to San Juan de la Peña, 10
Ayerbe, 19
Aznar II, count of Aragon, 6, 7
Aznar of Oteiza, 33
Aznar Pardo, 59, 60

Bahacalla, 22
Bailó, 76
Balaguer, 2, 71; city of, 59; conquest of, 48; castle of, 71
Banyoles, town of, 81; valley of, 79
Barbary, 71, 73
Barbastro, siege of, 48
Barbatuerta, 22
Barcelona, 42, 47, 53, 78, 81, 88, 95; assembly of, 47; cathedral of, 48; church of Friars Minor, 88, 97; city of, 80, 99, 101–3; county of, 49, 55, 102, 103; devastated by Muslims, 45; monastery of Friars Minor of, 103; new castle of, 85; origin of name, 2; Paupers' House, 50; royal palace, 88
Baux, family of, 52
Bellido Adolfo, 23
Belorado, settlement of, 25
Benedict, 6
Benedictine Order, 15, 26, 32, 39
Benifazá, monastery of, 65
Berdún, 76
Berenguer
    bishop of Girona, 46
    bishop-elect of Barcelona, 59
Berenguer Guillem, count of Cerdanya, 50
Berenguer Ramón
    I, count of Barcelona, 46, 47
    II, count of Barcelona, 47, 49
    marquis of Provence, 50, 52
Berlanga, settlement of, 25

Bernat I, "Trencaferre," count of Besalú, 45, 46
Bernat Centelles, 100
Bernat Guifred, count of Berguedá, 46
Bernat Guillem, count of Cerdanya, 48
Bernat Guillem
    II, count of Besalú, 48, 49
    III, count of Besalú, 50
Bernat Guillem Gras II, count of Besalú, 48
Bernat Guillem of Entença, 66
Bernat of Boxadors, 101
Bernat of Santa Eugenia, 78
Berroza, 5
Bertrán of Canellis, 95
Bertrán of Castelleto, 99
Bertrand Baus, 54
Bertrand of Ile, 76
Besalú, county of, 55
Betica, 1, 3
Béziers, 32, 59, 71
Bigorre, 8, 17
Bigüezal, 39
Blanche
    prioress of Sigena, 98
    of Anjou, wife of Jaime II of Aragon, 90, 91, 93, 95–98
Blasco, abbot of San Juan de la Peña, 17
Blasquita, daughter of Sancho Abarca, 12
Bocarove, 6
Bolea, conquest of, 19
Bonayre (Sardinia), 101
Boniface VIII, pope, 90, 91
Bordeaux, 74; seneschal of, 74
Borja, 37; assembly of, 31, 32; Pedro de Atarés, lord of, 31
Borja, river, 27
Borrell, count of Urgell, 44, 45
Bretó of Marseilles, 65
Briviesca, 13
Burgos, 13, 28, 30

Cadreita, 36, 39
Cagliari, castle of, 99, 101; cathedral of, 101; siege of, 100; tower of Orifany, 101
Calabria, 73
Calatayud, 37, 38, 40, 76; church of Friars Preacher in, 97; conquest of, 27
Calatrave, castle of, 59
Candespina, battle of, 28
Cantabria, 11, 12, 14

Carcassone, 59, 78; county of, 71
Carlet, papal legate, 79
Carmenzo, castle of, 78
Castan of Biel, 22, 24
Castelfabib, castle of, 59
Castella, conquest of, 20
Castellar above Zaragoza, 20, 26, 27
Castellon, viscounty of, 63
Castellón d'Ampurias, 78, 80
Castile, 14, 15, 19, 27, 28, 50, 89; county of, 13;
    kingdom of, 62; king of, 55, 96, 97
Catalunya, 42, 62
Cati, king of Carpetania, 1
Caxal, 35–38
Cecilia, countess of Urgell, 63
Celestine III, pope, 55
Celtiberia, 1, 2
Centule of Bearne, 26, 30
Cerdanya, count of, 66; county of, 55, 98
Cetubales, 1
Charles of Anjou, 69, 72–75, 78, 85
    king of Sicily, 69, 72, 73
Charles II of Anjou, 84, 85
    II, king of Naples, 89–93, 95, 96
    son of Charles of Anjou, 75
Charles of Valois, 79, 84, 86–88
    son of Philip III of France, 79
Cinca, river, 69
Cirauqui, 37
Citeaux, Order of, 66, 85
Ciurana, castle of, 51, 71, 85
Cluny, monastery of, 15
Colio, castle of, 54
Conflent, 41
Conrad, king of Sicily, 72
Constantinople, emperor of, 57, 62, 73, 92;
    empire of, 92
Constanza
    daughter of Jaime I, 63
    daughter of Jaime II of Aragon, 98
    daughter of Pedro III of Aragon, 84
    princess of Aragon, 55
    queen of Mallorca, 101
    wife of Pedro III of Aragon, 73
Córdoba, 30, 45; caliph of, 7; emir of, 5; king
    of, 30
Corsica, right of conquest of, 92
Corvino, conquest of, 19
Crevillente, 96
Cuenca, 24; battle of, 54

Cutanda, battle of, 27
Cyprus, king of, 98

Dalmacio, viscount of Rocabertí, 80, 99
Daroca, 37, 38, 40, 53; conquest of, 27
Denia, 30
Diego, count of Portell, 13
Diego of Vizcaya, 87
Dinis, king of Portugal, 96
Douce, countess of Barcelona, 49
Dubinaña, 13
Duero, river, 28

Ebro, river, 18, 30, 39, 51, 62
Eclipse of the sun, 2 February 1310, 97
Ejea, 25
Elche, 96
Elda, valley of, 96
Eleanora
    daughter of Sancho IV of Castile, 62
    daughter of Fernando IV of Castile, 97
    princess of Aragon, 55, 57
    wife of Alfonso IV of Aragon, 102, 103
Elisenda of Montcada, wife of Jaime II of
    Aragon, 99
Elne, city of, 79
Embrun, archbishop of, 90
England, king of, 55, 74, 87
Enric, son of Ramón Guifred, 48
Ermengol
    I, count of Urgell, 44–46
    II, Peregrín, count of Urgell, 46–48
    III, of Barbastro, count of Urgell, 48
    IV, of Gerp, count of Urgell, 48–50
    V, of Mallorca, count of Urgell, 50
    VI, of Castile, count of Urgell, 50, 51
    VII, count of Urgell, 56
    X, count of Urgell, 63, 71, 97
Ermisenda, wife of Ramiro I of Aragon, 17
Esteban, bishop of Jaca, 30
Estella, 20

Famine, 56
Fanlo, canonry of, 20
Federico
    governor in Sicily, 89, 91
    II, king of Sicily, 84, 91, 93, 94, 103
    son of Pedro III of Aragon, 73
Felicia, wife of Sancho Ramírez of Aragon,
    19

Fenollades, viscounty of, 71
Fernando
  I, king of Castile, 14, 15, 27
  IV, king of Castile, 92
  II, king of Leon, 58
  abbot of Montearagón, 55, 61
  marquis of Tortosa, 103
  son of Alfonso X of Castile, 70, 87
Fernando de la Cerda, grandson of Alfonso
  X of Castile, 87
Fernando Furtado, son of Gómez of Can-
  despina, 28
Fernando of Luna, 35
Fernando Sánchez of Castro, son of Jaime I,
  63, 69
Ferran, son of Jaume II of Mallorca, 98
Ferriz, 22
  of Huesca, 35
  of Lizana, 24, 35
Figueras, 78; royal palace of, 78
Fileu, son of Jaume II of Mallorca, 98
Filimer, Gothic king, 3
Filippo of Celucra, governor of Sardinia, 101
Flanders, 42
Foix, count of, 60, 70
Forcalquier, count of, 56, 58
Formigues, battle of, 80
Fortún
  abbot of San Juan de la Peña, 13
  bishop of Aragon, 10
  Maza, 22, 23
Fortún Garcés of Biel, 24
Fortún Garcés, king of Navarre, 7
Fortún Iñíguez of Let, 33
Fortún Jiménez, count of Aragon, 8, 9
Fraga, battle of, 29, 31; conquest of, 51
France, customs of, 60; king of, 41, 43, 60,
  73, 86
Frederick II Hohenstaufen, 57
Friars Minor, Order of, 65, 78, 88, 97, 98
Friars Preacher, Order of, 65

Gaderic, Gothic king, 3
Galberda, wife of Ramiro I of Aragon, 17
Galicia, 3, 29; origin of name, 1
Galindo II, count of Aragon, 7
Gallipienzo, 39
García
  bishop of Jaca, 17
  bishop of Zaragoza, 59
  son of Jimeno Garcés, 8
  V, king of Navarre, 33, 36–38
García d'Entrosiello, 22
García Iñíguez, king of Navarre, 6, 9
García Jiménez, king of Navarre, 6
García of Biduara, 35
García of Capra, count of Nájera, 22
García of Peña, 35
García Romeo, 59
García Sánchez
  I, king of Navarre, 13
  III, king of Navarre, 14, 15, 18
Gascons, 26
Gascony, 14, 22, 25, 60
Gaston of Bearne, 87
Gauceran of Sales, 56
Gavaldan, county of, 71
Geloira, wife of Sancho Garcés III of
  Navarre, 13, 16
Genoa, troops of, 51
Germany, emperor of, 52, 57, 62
Gerp, castle of, 48
Gil d'Atrosillo, 35
Gilbert, count of Provence, 49
Giovanni, duke of Athens, 103
Giron, king, 1
Girona, 49, 76, 78, 80–82; assembly at, 98;
  church of, 49; city of, 90; plaque in
  French army, 82; rebuilt, 84; reconquest
  of, 84; siege of, 81; surrender of the city,
  82
Gombau of Etença, 97
Gómez of Candespina, count of Castile, 28
Gómez of Luna, 22, 31, 35, 60
Gonzalo, count of Castile, 14–16, 22
Goths, 2
Granada, 30; king of, 77, 96, 97
Graus, 17
Gregory X, pope, 65
Guardamar, 96
Guifred, 41
  I, el Pilós, count of Barcelona, 41, 42
  II, count of Cerdanya, 45, 46
  son of Guifred I, count of Barcelona, 43
Guifred Guifred, archbishop of Narbonne,
  46
Guillaume VIII, baron of Montpellier, 57
Guillaume of Lodeve, admiral of France, 81

Guillelmo, son of Federico II of Sicily, 103
Guillelmo of Ferreris, papal legate, 90
Guillem, lord of Monteagudo, 100
Guillem Berenguer, count of Manresa, 47
Guillem Bernat Gras, I, count of Besalú, 46
Guillem Galceran, lord of Hostales, 68
Guillem Guifred, bishop of Urgell, 46
Guillem Jordán, count of Cerdanya, 48, 50
Guillem of Cardona, 59
Guillem of Cervera, 59
Guillem of Jossa, 80
Guillem of Pons, count of Urgell, 70
Guillem Olomar, burgess of Barcelona, 101
Guillem Ramón, count of Cerdanya, 48–50
Guillem Ramón of Odena, 69
Guillem Troyn, 48
Guillermo Aznárez of Oteiza, 33, 35
Guipúzcoa, 58
Guiraut of Cabrera, count of Urgell, 59, 63

Henry, son of Frederick II, 57
Hercules, 1, 2
Herrera, 38
Hesperia, 1
Hispania, origin of name, 2
Holy Cross, 67
Holy Land, 65
Honorius, Roman emperor, 3
Hospital of Jerusalem, Order of the, 61
Hostales, castle of, 68
Huc
    III, count of Ampurias, 63
    IV, count of Ampurias, 78
Huc of Santa Pau, 99
Huc of Totzo, admiral of Mallorca, 99
Huesca, 6, 19, 20, 24, 33, 34, 39; assembly of,
    34, 35, 37; bell of, 34; San Pedro el Viejo,
    church of, 39; conquest of, 23; siege of,
    20, 21, 27
Hugo, archbishop of Tarragona, 54
Hungary, king of, 55

Ibiza, conquest of, 65
Iglesia de Cixerri (Sardinia), siege and cap-
    ture of, 100
Iñigo, bishop of Aragon, 8
Iñigo Arista, king of Navarre, 8, 9
Iñigo of Aibar, 36
Innocent III, pope, 57

Irati, 39
Isabel
    daughter of Jaime II of Aragon, 98
    daughter of Jaume II of Mallorca, 98
    daughter of Pedro I of Aragon, 25
    queen of France, 63
Isabella, queen of Portugal, 84
Isidore of Seville, 1
Ispalis (Seville), 1
Ispan, bishop of Segovia, 61
Ispanus, 2

Jaca, 5, 17; canonry of, 20; city of, 87
Jaén, 62
Jaime
    I, king of the Crown of Aragon, 61–69
    II, king of the Crown of Aragon, 84, 88–
    94, 97, 98, 101–3
    II, king of Mallorca, 66, 68, 70, 71, 77, 79,
    85, 86, 89
    son of Jaime I, 62
    son of Jaime II of Aragon, 96, 97, 101, 102
    son of Pedro III of Aragon, 73, 75
Jaime de Figuera of Calatayud, 74
Jaime of Exerica, son of Jaime I, 63
Jaufre, viscount of Rocabertí, 63
Jaume
    II, king of Mallorca, 98
    III, king of Mallorca, 101, 102
    son of Jaume II, of Mallorca, 98
Javierre, 17
Jerusalem, 31, 48–50
Jews, 3
Jiménez of Artieda, castellan of Ull, 75
Jimeno Aznárez of Oteyza, 22
Jimeno Aznárez of Torres, 33, 35
Jimeno Cornel, 59
Jimeno d'Urrea, 92
Jimeno Garcés, king of Navarre, 8
Jimeno of Urrea, 93
John, cardinal-bishop of Santa Sabina, 62
John of Atarés, 6, 8
Juan, 93
    archbishop of Toledo, 97
    son of Alfonso IV of Aragon, 103
    son of Prince Manuel of Castile, 98
Juan de la Cerda, son of Alfonso X of Cas-
    tile, 93

Juan Jiménez of Urrea, lord of Monteagudo, 97
Juan Manuel, 98
Juan Nuñez de Lara, lord of Albarracín, 75
Júcar, river, 30
Julian, count, 4

Knights Templar, Order of, 59, 69

La Junquera, 83
La Muela, 96
La Peña del Cid, 24
Ladrón
    son of Iñigo Vélez, 22, 33, 35
    made count of Pamplona, 38
Las Navas de Tolosa, battle of, 59
Latre, 17
Lautres, viscountess of, 48
Lenzo, count of, 73
León, 14, 29; kingdom of, 58, 93
Leovigild, Gothic king, 3
Lérida, 50; archive of the cathedral of, 32;
    conquest of, 51; king of, 31; monastery
    of Friars Minor of, 103
Llorens, castle of, 59
Loarre, castle of, 15, 59
Logroño, peace conference at, 89
Lombardy, 52
Lope Ferrench of Luna, 22, 35, 59
Lope of Luna, count of Luna, 98
Los Arcos, battle of, 58
Louis
    VIII, king of France, 57
    IX, king of France, 63
    son of Charles of Valois, 88
Luchar, Muslim king, 24
Luna, 98; family of, 35; settlement of, 20
Lusitania, origin of name, 1
Lyon, city of, 65

Maguelonne, church of, 54
Mahon (Menorca), port of, 99
Mallorca, 50, 65; cathedral of, 64; city of, 49,
    64; conquest of, 61, 63, 64, 85; queen of,
    78
Mancio, bishop of Aragon, 15
Manfredo, count of Noratico, 100
Manrique, viscount of Narbonne, 77
Manuel, prince of Castile, 63

Marcellus, 6
Margarita, daughter of the count of Perche,
    38
Maria
    daughter of Jaime I, 63
    daughter of Jaime II of Aragon, 98
    daughter of Sancho IV of Castile, 89
    wife of Jaime II of Aragon, 98
    daughter of Sancho Abarca, 12
Marie of Montpellier, wife of Pedro II of
    Aragon, 58
Martin IV, pope, 72, 78
Matidero, 15
Mayor, wife of Sancho Garcés III of
    Navarre, 13, 15, 16
Maza, family of, 23
Menorca, conquest of, 64, 86, 87
Messina, 49, 73
Miguel Azlor, 35
Miguel of Luesia, 59, 60
Milhau, county of, 49, 71
Miramamolin, king, 59
Miravet, castle of, 51
Miró
    II, count of Barcelona, 43
    III, count of Besalú and bishop of Girona,
        44
Moncayo, origin of name, 1
Montclús, 16
Monteagudo, Juan Jiménez de Urrea, lord
    of, 97
Monteagudo de las Vicarias, 87
Montearagón, monastery of, 20, 21, 31, 55
Montes de Oca, 11, 15, 18
Montesa, castle of, 70
Montesquieu, castle of, 83
Montpellier, 66; barony of, 98; city of, 58;
    lord of, 66; lordship of, 71
Montroig, peace conference at, 90
Monzón, 31; assembly of, 33; castle of, 61;
    conquest of, 20
Monzón de Campos, 29
Morea and Tarentum, prince of, 98
Morella, battle of, 20
Moruel, castle of, 54
Muhammad, 3
Muñoz, count of Vizcaya, 12
Muradal, pass of, 59, 60
Murcia, 30; Aragonese conquest of, 92, 93;

cathedral of, 65; conquest of, 65; re-
  turned to Castile, 96; siege of, 64, 69
Muret, battle of, 60; castle of, 60
Muslim invasion, 4, 5

Nájera, 11, 13–15, 18
Naples, 75, 93–95
Narbonne, 41, 42; province of, 59
Natural lordship, 27, 62, 94
Navarre, 18, 19, 22, 33, 35, 39, 58
Nice, 53
Nicholas IV, pope, 88
Novella, valley of, 96
Nuño of Castile, 68

Ochorem, 37
Olea, family of, 28
Oliba, bishop of Vic, 45, 47
Oliba Cabreta, count of Cerdanya, 44
Oliver of Terme, 63
Onenga, wife of García Iníguez, king of
  Navarre, 10
Ordoña, 5
Ordoño
  II, king of Leon, 12
  king of Asturias, 7
Orihuela, 96
Oriol, bishop of Aragon, 12
Oristan (Sardinia), 99
Oroel, 5
Orunya, 25
Ostrogoths, 2
Oter de Humos, siege of, 93
Oto
  bishop of Barcelona, 46
  bishop of Girona, 46

Painted Rocks, 96
Palace, 88
Palamos, 93
Palamos, port of, 93
Palencia, 29
Palermo, 57; assembly at, 85; city of, 73
Pallars, count of, 48, 83; county of, 54, 55
Palma de Sols, port of, 100
Pamplona, 10, 12, 25, 31, 36; Muslim siege of,
  12; privileges of, 25
Panadés, 95

Panissars, pass of, 79–81; battle of, 83
Pano, 5
Paternus, abbot of San Juan de la Peña, 15
Pedro
  bishop of Zaragoza, 30
  brother of Jaime II of Aragon, 92, 93
  count of Ribagorza and Ampurias, 97, 102
  I, king of Aragon, 19–21, 24, 25
  II, king of the Crown of Aragon, 55–61,
    80, 82
  III, king of the Crown of Aragon, 66–75,
    77–79, 81, 84–86, 89, 102
  IV, king of the Crown of Aragon, 101, 103
  prince of Castile, 98
  son of Jaime I, 62
  son of Pedro I of Aragon, 25
  son of Pedro III of Aragon, 73, 84
Pedro Ahones, 62
Pedro Ansúrez, count of Castile, 27
Pedro Cornel, 35, 92
Pedro Fernández of Azagra, lord of Albarra-
  cín, 61, 92
Pedro Fernández of Ixer, son of Jaime I, 63
Pedro Martínez of Bolea, 76, 77
Pedro Martínez of Luna, 35
Pedro of Atarés, 31–33, 35
Pedro of Ayerbe, son of Jaime I, 63
Pedro of Lara, count of Castile, 28, 29
Pedro of Luesia, 35
Pedro of Moncayo, master of the Order of
  Knights Templar, 69
Pedro of Verga, 24
Pedro Pardo, 60
Pedro Rodríguez of Azagra, lord of Albarra-
  cín, 24
Pedro Tizón of Catareita, 31, 32
Pedro Vergua, 35
Pelayo, 5
Perche, count of, 26, 27, 38
Pere, bishop of Vic, 54
Pere of Moncada, 63
Pere Ramón, son of Ramón Berenguer I, 47
Peregrín of Castillazuelo, 32
Perelada, town of, 80
Perpignan, 56, 70, 77, 79, 83, 90; church of
  Friars Minor of, 90
Pertica del Astor, 49
Peter, papal legate, 61
Petilla, 15, 17

Petronilla, wife of Ramón Berenguer IV, 38, 51, 52
Philip
    III, king of France, 63, 71, 74, 79–82, 84
    IV, king of France, 79
Piedra Pisada, battle of, 19
Pietro II, king of Sicily, 103
Pina, burned by Muslims, 19
Pintano, valley of, 76
Pisa, 49, 101; commune of, 99–101
Plague, 93, 97
Poblet, monastery of, 65–68, 70
Poitiers, count of, 27, 34
Pons Guillem, 78
Pons Huc I, count of Ampurias, 63, 78
Pons of Cabrera, count of Urgell, 63
Pons of Guardia, governor of Mallorca, 85
Pons of Ribellas, 71
Pons, castle of, 70
Portell, county of, 13
Portfangós, 71, 99
Portugal, 14, 29; king of, 84, 93; prince of, 65
Pratiella, conquest of, 19
Privileges of Aragon, 83, 84, 86, 87, 103
Provence, 17, 58; county of, 49, 52, 54, 55, 58
Ptolemy, 2
Puente de la Reina, 37
Purification of the Blessed Mary, feast of, 97

Quarto Sant'Elena (Sardinia), 99

Radegaisus, Gothic king, 3
Radulfo
    bishop of Urgell, 43
    monk of Ripoll, 43
Ramiro
    bishop of Barbastro and Roda, 32
    bishop of Burgos, 32
    bishop of Pamplona, 32
    I, king of Aragon, 14, 16–18, 27
    II, king of Aragon, 19, 31–33, 35–39, 51, 53
    II, king of Leon, 12
    prince of Navarre, 18
Ramón
    count of Barcelona, 45
    prince of Navarre, 18, 33
    viscount of Villamur, 71
Ramón Berenguer
    count of Prades, 98, 102

count of Provence, 53
    I, count of Barcelona, 47
    II, count of Barcelona, 47
    III, count of Barcelona, 49
    IV, count of Barcelona, 38–40, 50, 51
    IV, count of Provence, 56
Ramón Folch
    count of Ampurias, 59
    count of Cardona, 83
    viscount of Cardona, 71, 80, 82
Ramón Guifred, count of Cerdanya, 46, 48
Ramón Marquet, 80
Ramón of Anglesola, 71, 80
Ramón of Cardona, 63
Ramón of Fores, 35
Ramón Roger, count of Pallars, 71
Ramónat of Gascony, 16
Raymond
    count of Toulouse, 28, 37, 53–55
    VI, count of Toulouse, 57
    VII, count of Toulouse, 57
Recared, Gothic king, 3
Rhone, river, 46, 52, 54, 65
Ribagorza, 5, 16
Ripoll, monastery of, 43, 44, 46, 48, 50, 52; altars, 47; rebuilding of, 45, 47
Robert
    king of Sicily and Jerusalem, 84
    son of Charles of Valois, 88
    son of Charles of Salerno, 92
Robert Guiscard, duke of Apulia and Messina, 49
Robert of Anjou, king of Naples, 98
Rocabertí, viscount of, 99
Roderic, Gothic king, 4
Rodrigo Díaz, the Cid, 17, 18, 20, 23, 24, 33
Rodrigo Vicarra, 77
Roger, count of Foix, 63
Roger Bernard, count of Foix, 71
Roger de Lauria, 74, 75, 81, 83
Roman liturgy, 19
Rome, 57, 58, 92, 93
Roncal, 36, 39
Rosas, 80; monastery of the town of, 83; naval battle of, 81
Rosselló, county of, 54, 55, 66, 79, 90
Rotrou, count of Perche, 26, 27, 38
Rueda, massacre in, 19
Ruesta, 15, 17

Ruy Jiménez of Luna, 35

Saint Agatha, feast of, 8
Saint Bartholomew, feast of, 96
Saint Basilissa, 8
Saint Benedict, 15
Saint Clement, 8
Saint Dalmatia, burg of Turin, 52
Saint Felix, 6; church of, 81
Saint George, 23, 66
Saint Indalecio, translation of, 19
Saint James of Urtie (Algeciras), translation of, 19
Saint Jerome, 1
Saint John the Baptist, 8; feast of, 20
Saint Julián, 8
Saint Mary, 66
Saint Mary of the Knights of the Temple of Jerusalem, Order of, 50
Saint Michael, 8; feast of, 64
Saint Narcissus, relic of, 81
Saint Pancras, church of, 57
Saint Peter, church of, 58
Saint Petronilla, altar of, 58
Saint Pons of Thomières, monastery of, 19, 32, 34, 39
Saint Sylvester, feast of, 64
Saint Voto, 6
Salazar, 39
Salerno, 72
Salomó, count of Barcelona, 42
Salvatierra, castle of, 76
Samitier, 15
San Facundo and Primitivo, monastery of, 32
San Jorge de la Boqueras, church of, 23
San Juan de la Peña, monastery of, 5, 7, 9, 10, 12, 13, 17, 21, 25, 39; Blasco, abbot of, 17; Fortún, abbot of, 13; Paternus, abbot of, 15; Sancho, abbot of, 19; Transirico, abbot of, 8; Transmiro, abbot of, 12; altars of, 8; archives of, 25, 36, 58; donations to, 9, 10, 20, 25, 26; foundation of, 6; privileges of, 10; relics of, 19; Roman rite introduced in, 19; transferred to Benedictines, 15
San Lorenzo, castle of, 63
San Marco, cape of, 99
San Martín (Sardinia), 101

San Martín, bridge of, 39
San Martín de Cercito, monastery of, 7
San Pedro de Siresa, monastery of, 39
San Pedro in Huesca, church of, 39
San Salvador de Leire, monastery of, 9, 36–39
San Salvador de Oña, monastery of, 15
San Victorián de Sobrarbe, monastery of, 16, 39
Sanç
    count of Rosselló, 61, 62
    king of Mallorca, 98, 99, 101
Sança, daughter of Jaume II of Mallorca, 98
Sancha
    daughter of Ramiro I, king of Aragon, 17
    princess of Aragon, 55
    wife of Alfonso II of Aragon, 54, 60
    daughter of Sancho Abarca, 12
Sancho, 33, 52
    abbot of San Juan de la Peña, 19
    archbishop of Toledo, 62, 68
    bishop of Pamplona, 13
    count of Castile, 13
    count of Rosselló and Cerdanya, 52
    count, son of Alfonso VI of Castile, 20
    I, king of Portugal, 52
    II, king of Castile, 17, 23, 24, 30
    II, king of Leon and Castile, 18
    IV, king of Castile, 62, 87, 89, 90
    VI, king of Navarre, 58
    pueyo de, 21
Sancho Abarca, town in Cantabria, 12
Sancho Fontana, 35
Sancho Garcés
    I (Abarca), king of Navarre, 7, 10–12
    III, king of Navarre, 13–15, 27, 36
    IV, king of Navarre, 17, 18, 30, 33
Sancho of Antillon, 63
Sancho of Larrosa, bishop of Pamplona, 33, 36, 37
Sancho of Peña, 22
Sancho Ramírez
    chronicle of, 33
    I, king of Aragon, 17–21, 27, 32
    illegitimate son of Ramiro I of Aragon, 17
Sant Benet de Bagés, monastery of, 47
Sant Celoni, 19
Sant Martí de Canigó, monastery of, 46
Santa Engracia de Puerto, 39

Santa Eulalia, reconquest of, 20
Santa María del Pilar, 26
Santa María del Puig, 41, 66
Santas Creus, monastery of, 85, 102
Santiago de Compostela, pilgrimage route
    to, 13, 56
Sanz Berenguer, prior of Sant Benet de
    Bagés, 47
Sarassa of Navarre, family of, 76
Sardinia, 102; right of conquest of, 92; Ara-
    gonese invasion of, 99
Sarisa, 36
Sauve Majeur, monastery of, 25, 26
Segorbe, 98
Segovia, 2
    Ispan, bishop of, 61
Sepúlveda, 28
Sicily, 72, 95; emissaries of, 91; king of, 57;
    kingdom of, 78; revolt in, 73
Sigena, monastery of, 60, 98; foundation of,
    54
Simon, count of Montfort, 59–61
Sisebut, Gothic king, 3
Sobrarbe, 5, 14–16, 18
Soria, 27, 55; settlement of, 25
Spelunca de Guallons, donation to San Juan
    de la Peña, 9
Stantia (Scandia), 2
Suinthila, Gothic king, 3
Sunifred
    II, count of Urgell, 43, 44
    II, count of Cerdanya and Besalú, 44

Tagello, castle of, 65
Tarazona, 37, 38, 40, 53, 75; assembly of, 62;
    conquest of, 27; origin of name, 1; peace
    conference at, 96
Tarragona, 99; archbishop of, 89; bishop of,
    65
Tauste, conquest of, 26
Teresa
    daughter of Ramiro I, king of Aragon, 17
    wife of Jaime II of Aragon, 99, 101, 103
Teresa Gil of Bidaura, 63
Teruel, city of, 62; repopulation of, 54
Tet, river, 41
Toda
    wife of Iñigo Arista, king of Navarre, 9
    wife of Sancho Garcés I and queen of
        Navarre, 12

Toledan liturgy (Mozarabic rite), 19
Toledo, 3, 20, 24, 25, 27, 37
Torricella, fief of, 78; castle of, 78
Tortosa, 50, 51; cathedral of, 51; conquest of,
    51
Toulouse, 3, 7, 17, 61; city of, 55; count of, 60;
    countesses of, 59; seneschal of, 75
Transirico, abbot of San Juan de la Peña, 8
Transmiro, abbot of San Juan de la Peña, 12
Trapani, city of, 73
Trencataya, castle of, 52
Trial by combat, 14, 74, 75
Tripoli, 50
Troncedo, 15
Tubal, 1
Tudela, 12, 26, 27, 37–39; conquest of, 26
Turin, 52
Turks, 50

Ubeda, battle of, 59
Ugo
    judge of Arborea and viscount of Basso,
        99
    papal legate, 47
Ull, castle of, 75
Urban II, pope, 25
Urgell, 2; count of, 70, 71; county of, 103
Urraca
    wife of Alfonso I of Aragon, 25, 27, 28, 37
    daughter of Sancho Abarca, 12
    queen of Navarre, 6
    See Petronilla
Usatges of Barcelona, 47

Vadoluengo, 15, 39; treaty of, 35
Valdonsella, 75
Valencia, 18, 30, 33, 50, 56, 66, 78, 102, 103; ca-
    thedral of, 64, 68; city of, 62; conquest
    of, 24, 61, 63, 64, 69; kingdom of, 65,
    102, 103; siege of, 64; uprising in, 69, 70
Valens, Roman emperor, 3
Vallverde, church of, 65
Valtierra, 36, 39
Vergs, castle of, 78
Verig, Gothic king, 2
Veruela, monastery of, 62
Viadongos, battle of, 29
Viana, 18
Vilabertrán, 91
Vilar Estarrat, 78

Villafranca del Panadés, 85
Violant
    daughter of Jaime I of Aragon, 62, 65
    daughter of Pedro III of Aragon, 92
    daughter of Jaime II of Aragon, 98
Violant (Andrea), queen of the Crown of
        Aragon, 62
Visigoths, 2
Vitoria, 20, 33, 58
Vizcaya, 5

Wallia, Gothic king, 3

Wamba, Gothic king, 4
William Bertrand, count of Provence, 17
Witiza, Gothic king, 4

Zamora, 23
Zaragoza, 21, 37, 38, 40, 51, 53; assembly at,
        70, 84, 89, 86, 102; city of, 101; conquest
        of, 27; Count of Alperche Street, 27;
        Friars Minor, chapter house of, 93;
        Santa María del Pilar, 27; siege of, 26
Zuera, 22

University of Pennsylvania Press
MIDDLE AGES SERIES
Edward Peters, General Editor

David Anderson. *Before the Knight's Tale: Imitation of Classical Epic in Boccaccio's Teseida*. 1988

J. M. W. Bean. *From Lord to Patron: Lordship in Late Medieval England*. 1990

Uta-Renate Blumenthal. *The Investiture Controversy: Church and Monarchy from the Ninth to the Twelfth Century*. 1988

Daniel Bornstein, trans. *Dino Compagni's Chronicle of Florence*. 1986

Betsy Bowden. *Chaucer Aloud: The Varieties of Textual Interpretation*. 1987

James William Brodman. *Ransoming Captives in Crusader Spain: The Order of Merced on the Christian-Islamic Frontier*. 1986

Robert I. Burns, S.J., ed. *Emperor of Culture: Alfonso X the Learned of Castile and His Thirteenth-Century Renaissance*. 1990

David Burr. *Olivi and Franciscan Poverty: The Origins of the* Usus Pauper *Controversy*. 1989

Thomas M. Cable. *The English Alliterative Tradition*. 1991

Leonard Cantor, ed. *The English Medieval Landscape*. 1982

Anthony K. Cassell and Victoria Kirkham, eds. and trans. *Diana's Hunt. Caccia di Diana. Boccaccio's First Fiction*. 1991

Willene B. Clark and Meradith T. McMunn, eds. *Beasts and Birds of the Middle Ages: The Bestiary and Its Legacy*. 1989

G. G. Coulton. *From St. Francis to Dante: Translations from the Chronicle of the Franciscan Salimbene (1221–1288)*. 1972

Richard C. Dales. *The Scientific Achievement of the Middle Ages*. 1973

Charles T. Davis. *Dante's Italy and other Essays*. 1984

George T. Dennis, trans. *Maurice's Strategikon: Handbook of Byzantine Military Strategy*. 1984

Katherine Fischer Drew, trans. *The Burgundian Code: The Book of the Constitutions or Law of Gundobad and Additional Enactments*. 1972

Katherine Fischer Drew, trans. *Laws of the Salian Franks*. 1991

Katherine Fischer Drew, trans. *The Lombard Laws*. 1973

Nancy Edwards. *The Archaeology of Early Medieval Ireland*. 1990

Margaret J. Ehrhart. *The Judgment of the Trojan Prince Paris in Medieval Literature*. 1987

Patrick J. Geary. *Aristocracy in Provence: The Rhône Basin at the Dawn of the Carolingian Age*. 1985

Julius Goebel, Jr. *Felony and Misdemeanor: A Study in the History of Criminal Law*. 1976

Avril Henry, ed. *The Mirour of Mans Saluacione*. 1987

J. N. Hillgarth. *Christianity and Paganism, 350–750: The Conversion of Western Europe.* 1986

Richard C. Hoffmann. *Land, Liberties, and Lordship in a Late Medieval Countryside: Agrarian Structures and Change in the Duchy of Wrocław.* 1990

Robert Hollander. *Boccaccio's Last Fiction: "Il Corbaccio."* 1988

Edward B. Irving, Jr. *Rereading* Beowulf. 1989

C. Stephen Jaeger. *The Origins of Courtliness: Civilizing Trends and the Formation of Courtly Ideals, 939–1210.* 1985

William Chester Jordan. *The French Monarchy and the Jews: From Philip Augustus to the Last Capetians.* 1989

William Chester Jordan. *From Servitude to Freedom: Manumission in the Sénonais in the Thirteenth Century.* 1986

Ellen E. Kittell. *From* Ad Hoc *to Routine: A Case Study in Medieval Bureaucracy.* 1991

Alan C. Kors and Edward Peters, eds. *Witchcraft in Europe, 1000–1700: A Documentary History.* 1972

Jeanne Krochalis and Edward Peters, eds. and trans. *The World of Piers Plowman.* 1975

E. Ann Matter. *The Voice of My Beloved: The Song of Songs in Western Medieval Christianity.* 1990

María Rosa Menocal. *The Arabic Role in Medieval Literary History.* 1987

A. J. Minnis. *Medieval Theory of Authorship.* 1988

Lawrence Nees. *A Tainted Mantle: Hercules and the Classical Tradition at the Carolingian Court.* 1991

Lynn H. Nelson, trans. *The Chronicle of San Juan de la Peña: A Fourteenth-Century Official History of the Crown of Aragon.* 1991

Charlotte A. Newman. *The Anglo-Norman Nobility in the Reign of Henry II: The Second Generation.* 1988

Thomas F. X. Noble. *The Republic of St. Peter: The Birth of the Papal State, 680–825.* 1984

Joseph F. O'Callaghan. *The Cortes of Castile-León, 1188–1350.* 1989

William D. Paden, ed. *The Voice of the Trobairitz: Perspectives on the Women Troubadours.* 1989

Kenneth Pennington. *Popes and Bishops. The Papal Monarchy in the Twelfth and Thirteenth Centuries.* 1989

Edward Peters. *The Magician, the Witch, and the Law.* 1982

Edward Peters, ed. *Christian Society and the Crusades, 1198–1229.* Sources in Translation, including The Capture of Damietta by Oliver of Paderborn. 1971

Edward Peters, ed. *The First Crusade: The Chronicle of Fulcher of Chartres and Other Source Materials.* 1971

Edward Peters, ed. *Heresy and Authority in Medieval Europe.* 1980

Edward Peters, ed. *Monks, Bishops, and Pagans: Christian Culture in Gaul and Italy, 500–700.* 1975

Clifford Peterson. *Saint Erkenwald.* 1977

James M. Powell. *Anatomy of a Crusade, 1213–1221.* 1986

Donald E. Queller. *The Fourth Crusade: The Conquest of Constantinople, 1201–1204.* 1977

Michael Resler, trans. *EREC by Hartmann von Aue*. 1987

Pierre Riché (Jo Ann McNamara, trans.). *Daily Life in the World of Charlemagne*. 1978

Jonathan Riley-Smith. *The First Crusade and the Idea of Crusading*. 1986

Barbara H. Rosenwein. *Rhinoceros Bound: Cluny in the Tenth Century*. 1982

Steven Sargent, ed. and trans. *On the Threshold of Exact Science: Selected Writings of Anneliese Maier on Late Medieval Natural Philosophy*. 1982

Robert Somerville and Kenneth Pennington, eds. *Law, Church, and Society: Essays in Honor of Stephan Kuttner*. 1977

Susan Mosher Stuard, ed. *Women in Medieval History and Historiography*. 1987

Susan Mosher Stuard, ed. *Women in Medieval Society*. 1976

Ronald E. Surtz. *The Guitar of God: Gender, Power, and Authority in the Visionary World of Mother Juana de la Cruz (1481–1534)*. 1990

Patricia Terry, trans. *Poems of the Elder Edda*. 1990

Frank Tobin. *Meister Eckhardt: Thought and Language*. 1986

Ralph Turner. *Men Raised from the Dust: Administrative Service and Upward Mobility in Angevin England*. 1988

Harry Turtledove, trans. *The Chronicle of Theophanes: An English Translation of* anni mundi *6095–6305 (A.D. 602–813)*. 1982

Mary F. Wack. *Lovesickness in the Middle Ages: The* Viaticum *and Its Commentaries*. 1990

Benedicta Ward. *Miracles and the Medieval Mind: Theory, Record, and Event, 1000–1215*. 1982

Suzanne Fonay Wemple. *Women in Frankish Society: Marriage and the Cloister, 500–900*. 1981.

This book has been set in Linotron Galliard. Galliard was designed for Mergenthaler in 1978 by Matthew Carter. Galliard retains many of the features of a sixteenth century typeface cut by Robert Granjon but has some modifications which gives it a more contemporary look.

Printed on acid-free paper.